PRAISE FOR RODNEY SAULSBERRY

"Rodney Saulsberry knows there are no shortcuts to success in voiceover. Basics are key, and that starts with preparation. In this, his third book for VO students, Saulsberry gets you ready for the most challenging copy with the proper mouth exercises."

—DAVE COURVOISIER, NEWS ANCHOR, VOICE ACTOR

"I'm thrilled to be part of your Consultant's Club. The one-on-one sessions with you, and also the group conference calls have been extremely beneficial! Working with you is invaluable and has helped to bolster my confidence in my abilities as a voice artist. Thank you for sharing your gifts and talents. And thank you for being so encouraging."

—EVELYN CLARKE, VOICE ACTOR

"I joined the Consultant's Club in October 2013. It has been one of the best decisions I have made thus far! Being a member of the Consultant's Club has improved my ability to read, interpret, and deliver copy. Most importantly, I have gained more confidence than I have ever had. In addition to honing my voiceover skills, being a member has taught me marketing, vocal care, script analysis, and much more with the monthly calls from featured guests. Rodney has been a huge help and has guided me along my journey. I am so thankful to have been a part of the Consultant's Club. Thank you, Rodney!"

—TONYA SIMMONS, VO ACTOR

"I'm a member of the Consultant's Club and attended Rodney's New York Commercial Intensive Voice Over Workshop! in November. The class was a real game changer for me, it got me motivated to work harder, practice more and learn all I could about this wonderful industry. The lessons I learned about interpreting copy and putting them into practice were instrumental in my landing a new gig on Voices.com after having been a member for just over a month. Rodney thanks for your guidance, inspiration and expertise "

—BILL CLINE, VO ACTOR

"Working with Rodney Saulsberry was an absolute joy on what could have been a very difficult project. I had written a documentary and I needed an announcer who could read this serious copy while at the same time letting the audience feel comfortable about laughing at it. That's the kind of performance you can't really coax out of someone. Either they have it or they don't.

"Rodney came in and gave me everything I could have hoped for. Not only that, he was positive, funny, up for anything, and he truly seemed to enjoy playing and experimenting with the performance. When he left, I turned to the engineer and said, 'Boy, did we luck out.'"

—ANDY BOBROW, WRITER, *Malcolm in the Middle*

TONGUE TWISTERS
and
VOCAL WARM-UPS

OTHER BOOKS FROM TOMDOR PUBLISHING

Step Up to the Mic: A Positive Approach to Succeeding in Voice-Overs

You Can Bank on Your Voice: Your Guide to a Successful Career in Voice-Overs (paperback and audio)

RODNEY SAULSBERRY'S
TONGUE TWISTERS

and

VOCAL WARM-UPS

with

OTHER VOCAL-CARE TIPS

Copyright © 2015 by Rodney Saulsberry

All rights reserved. No part of this book may be reproduced in any manner or form whatsoever, by any means, electronically or mechanically, including photocopying or recording, or by any information or retrieval system, without the expressed written permission from the publisher, except by a reviewer, who may quote brief passages for reviews or articles about the book.

TOMDOR PUBLISHING

P. O. Box 1735
Agoura Hills, CA 91376-1735
Tel: 818-207-2682
Email: rodtalks@pacbell.net

ISBN: 978-0-9747678-2-6
Library of Congress Control Number: 2015905260

Printed in the United States of America

Cover design by Kristine Mills
Back cover photo by Lorenzo Diggins Jr.
Author photo on page 185 by Jennifer Manley
Text design and layout by Mary Jo Zazueta

To the members of my Consultant's Club. Thank you for the honor of helping you fulfill your voiceover dreams.

Contents

	Foreword	11
	Acknowledgments	13
	Introduction	15

Section 1: Tongue Twisters

CHAPTER 1	The Value of Tongue Twisters	19
CHAPTER 2	Popular YouTube Twisters	29
CHAPTER 3	Warm-Ups Before and During a Session	36
CHAPTER 4	Fast Tags	42
CHAPTER 5	Movie Trailer Legal Tags	50
CHAPTER 6	Spoken Word Tongue Twisters	52

Section 2: Voiceover Challenges

CHAPTER 7	Mouth Noises and Other Issues	63
CHAPTER 8	Blended Sounds	74
CHAPTER 9	Punctuation	79
CHAPTER 10	A Spanish Tongue Twister	82
CHAPTER 11	Avoid "Announcer" Delivery	84
CHAPTER 12	Roadblocks	87
CHAPTER 13	Video-Game Voiceover	89

Section 3: Vocal Warm-Ups

CHAPTER 14	Exercising Facial Muscles	99
CHAPTER 15	Getting the Most from Vocal Warm-Ups	101
CHAPTER 16	The Ramp-Up … and the Groove	109
CHAPTER 17	Personalization	115

Section 4: Mic Technique & Other Tips

CHAPTER 18	Getting the Most from the Mic	119
CHAPTER 19	Vocal Care	123
CHAPTER 20	Allergies and Sinus Care	127

Section 5: More Tongue Twisters

CHAPTER 21	Twisters for Specific Genres	135
CHAPTER 22	Twisters and Warm-Ups for Singers	151
CHAPTER 23	Prepare for Your Next Speech	154

Section 6: Enhance Your Voiceover Career

CHAPTER 24	Building a Successful Career	159
CHAPTER 25	Setting Career Goals	166
CHAPTER 26	Be a Winner	171
	Glossary	179
	Bibliography and References	183
	About the Author	185
	Join the Consultant's Club	187
	I Want to Hear from You	189

Foreword

OCTOBER 1999. IT WAS MY FIRST DAY AS A CLIENT at the William Morris Agency in Beverly Hills. I was excited beyond belief at the prospect of mounting a career in LA as a voice-over professional. I can never seem to shake the insecurities of calling myself a voiceover professional. To this day, I don't believe I've come close to mastering the craft. There are only a few, in my mind who have. One in particular.

The waiting room at the agency seemed to be a who's who of voiceover movers and shakers and I felt like a little child out of my element. Of all the new faces and voices I recall from that day, one stood out. A giant of a man with a voice just as big—and as smooth as warm Nutella. Rodney Saulsberry. I liked him right away. Hell, he was giving me a back massage with his voice as I leaned up against the wall. Every time he spoke, the wall seemed to vibrate. Kind of like massage machines in airports. Try one next time you're traveling. You'll get the idea.

There was also wisdom in his voice and I was drinking it in. It became a regular routine as I became a more regular client. We'd exchange hellos and good-byes with a little conversation thrown in as we were brought in to read that day's auditions.

Over the years, I came to know Rodney better. I quickly realized what a pro he was—and an amazing talent. He is extremely passionate about his craft and always working on it.

The greatest thing about Rodney Saulsberry is his

pay-it-forward attitude. He is giving us this gift. A peek into the wonderful world of voice. There is no easy way to get into the business of voiceover. There are no shortcuts. Today, with everyone having access to a microphone and a computer you better be damned good right out of the gate. Just getting an agent to listen can be like trying to set up base camp at Mt Everest. In a blizzard!

But if you are truly, wholeheartedly, and absolutely 100 percent sure this is what you want to do, then you need to prepare and work. Rodney's first two books, *You Can Bank on Your Voice* and *Step Up to the Mic* are pretty much required reading. *Tongue Twisters and Vocal Warm-Ups* will also be invaluable to you as you start your journey.

And, if you are already a working pro, this book is gold. Especially if you're switching gears from one session to the next during the day. There are many fabulous tips in here that WORK! This book will be at my side in the studio every day.

I am honored to write this foreword for Rodney. It's quite surreal, actually. I love this business and the people in it—and we should all be thankful that Rodney Saulsberry has given us his voice.

I love you, man. Thank you and continued success.

David Kaye, Voice Actor

Acknowledgments

Once again, I am grateful for the team of professionals who helped me put together my third book. The process of writing a book is definitely not an easy one. I could not have done it if I wasn't passionate about the subject matter.

Also, thank you to everyone who has joined my Consultant's Club. Your decision to seek my knowledge and consultation has inspired me more than you will ever know.

Introduction

WHEN I TRAVEL AROUND THE COUNTRY HOSTING workshops and other voiceover events, people don't greet me with an extended hand followed by a hello. They extend their hand, and with a big smile from ear to ear, they recite one of my many tongue twisters. The most popular being "Why in the world would a whale want water? When a whale wants water will a well run dry?" I am flattered by the recognition of my work from voiceover actors all over the world and it has inspired me to write this, my third book.

Every profession that requires physicality requires proper exercise, warm-up, and preparation for the task at hand—and tongue twisters are the perfect warm-up for your voice. Every time you do one of the tongue twisters in this book, you will have just performed a complex dance with many body parts, including your lips, tongue, jaw, and larynx that will quickly get you ready to read copy.

As any of my students will attest, I believe that voiceover is analogous to music and that when you read a piece of copy you are singing a song. The difference in the way you sing that song compared to another performer is in its interpretation. In voiceover, the punctuation and the VO direction are the music notes. To do well as a voice artist, you must find the music in all scripts and tongue twisters.

People don't speak in one cadence. Our everyday speech is rhythmic. It's like singing notes. We vary our rhythms based on intent. If we want to drive a point home, we may speed up our tempo. If we want to stretch out a point, we may slow down our tempo. When you start that musical journey with a rhythmic tongue twister, your journey to success begins.

This book is designed to help anyone who uses his or her voice for business. It will help voiceover professionals perfect reading exactly what is on the page with the flair and dexterity that is needed to read fast tags, medical copy, animation, promos, narration, video games, audiobooks, trailers, and commercial copy.

Toastmasters International members will find this book to be helpful in preparing them for speaking events that could lead to a Golden Gavel Award or a World Championship! Teachers of speech and diction will find this book useful in the classroom, and public speakers will keep it right next to their prepared text as a warm-up vehicle before every speech! If you are about to use your voice to communicate to others on any professional level, this is the book for you.

And, finally, *Tongue Twisters and Vocal Warm-Ups* will also benefit singers.

All of the tongue twisters and vocal warm-ups in this book, except where indicated, were written by me. Many of my YouTube favorites are included, along with many new and challenging creations. Also included is a section on how to enhance your voiceover career, because if you have the confidence and discipline to practice tongue twisters, then you have the tools to pursue success in the voiceover world.

Keep this book with you at all times and have fun as you improve your skills and elevate your voice career. *Tongue Twisters and Vocal Warm-Ups* gives you everything you need to perform at your highest peak every time you step up to the mic.

Ready? Let's get started!

Section 1

Tongue Twisters

> "Why in the world would a whale want water, when a whale wants water will a well run dry?"
> –RODNEY SAULSBERRY

CHAPTER **1**

The Value of Tongue Twisters

TONGUE TWISTERS ARE A GROUP OF WORDS THAT ARE designed for practicing pronunciation and to gain fluency in whatever you are about to do vocally. It should also be noted that my tongue twisters are neither grammatically correct nor necessarily meaningful. They are simply tools to get you warmed up before speaking or singing.

Experts agree that tongue twisters: 1) stimulate memory, focus and concentration; 2) improve your listening perception and comprehension; 3) increase your speech speed; 4) help you speak with precision and no mistakes; and 5) entertain both children and adults while learning.

A tongue twister is a phrase that is designed to be difficult to articulate properly. Consider:

"Forget Peter Piper and his Peck of Pickled Pepper—psychologists have come up with what may be the world's most

frustrating tongue twister. It may not make much sense, but the phrase 'pad kid poured curd pulled cold' completely defeated volunteers taking part in a U.S. speech study. Asked to repeat the phrase 10 times at a fast lick, many of the participants clammed up and stopped talking altogether, according to lead researcher Dr. Stefanie Shattuck-Hufnagel, from Massachusetts Institute of Technology (MIT) in Boston. ... The tongue twister study, presented at the annual meeting of the Acoustical Society of America in San Francisco, was conducted to shed light on the brain's speech-planning processes."

—"Can YOU Say 'Pad Kid Poured Curd Pulled Cold'?" *The Daily Mail* [UK], December 4, 2013

I absolutely dare you to say this well-known twister five times fast and clearly:

Toy boat, toy boat, toy boat, toy boat, toy boat.

USE YOUR HANDS

I use my hands quite often when I do voiceovers. It's all a part of my music within every word that I speak. My hands denote rhythm. My hands denote melody. I am a conductor and I am conducting my symphony of words. My voice is my instrument and I am in control of it. My hand movements are in conjunction with the words that I speak, first in my tongue twister warm-up and it continues when I read the copy.

Every piece of copy is different and it requires a different beat in your voice. Tongue twisters differ in beat and can prepare you for your next session or audition.

Here are seven reasons why tongue twisters and vocal warm-ups are so important to voiceover artists:

1. **Concentration**. You cannot read a tongue twister and be successful in comprehending it and speaking it correctly without concentrating. This effort before you read voiceover or speech copy gets you in the mold and mood for concentrating on your prepared text.

2. **Articulation**. Tongue twisters help you articulate long sentences without stumbling and they help you string together difficult sounds without slurring.

3. **Enunciation**. Tongue twisters help you speak more clearly. They help you achieve better diction.

4. **Rhythm**. It takes a good sense of rhythm to read voiceover copy. Tongue twisters are almost exclusively rhythmic.

5. **Pronunciation**. Tongue twisters improve your pronunciation of words, which is paramount for voiceover.

6. **Mouth Muscles**. Tongue twisters strengthen the muscles necessary for proper speech. The exaggerated way that you have to move your lips, jaws, and tongue while reading a tongue twister is very helpful for reading tough copy.

7. **Eye-Word-Mouth**. Tongue twisters get you in the habit of using what I call the Eye-Word-Mouth method. Let's break it down. *Eye*, first you see it. *Word*, you see and internalize the words. *Mouth*, you let the words come out of your mouth without stumbling.

Since the beginning of time, humans have been faced with the need to exert a certain amount of energy to live from day to day. The earliest inhabitants had to hunt for food with weapons far less powerful than what we have today. As technology continues to make present-day conditions easier for all of us, the one thing that remains constant is the need to practice to become better at what you do.

If you start a voiceover session that is obviously going to require shouting and long hours, you have to warm-up properly. If you are going to read fast tags and wordy legal disclaimers, you need to read tongue twisters that embody the types of words and language that you are about to read.

Do you have a promo session or audition coming up? Practice the promo tongue twisters. Want to warm up for a narration audition or job? Do a long-form spoken word tongue twister. How about a trailer vocal warm-up?

Practice, practice, practice and more practice is the way to success.

TONGUE TWISTERS PROMOTE CONCENTRATION

When it comes to voiceover, tongue twisters are very important. Not just because they challenge you but also because they require your undivided attention at all times to comprehend what it takes to deliver them properly; which is the same thing that is required when you read voiceover copy.

When I coach students, I always start the session off with a number of reasonably difficult tongue twisters. These tongue twisters take a better-than-average ability to execute. By doing these twisters first, before we start to read copy, the student enters a mode of concentration that translates inevitably to the copy.

IT'S NOT ALWAYS A MATTER OF SPEED

If you are reading fast tags, or if you have been directed to speak at a fast pace, it is okay to read fast. But speed is not the intent of the tongue twister. Sure, speed is impressive and it's a lot of fun to read fast. However, the true intent of the tongue twister is to promote mental gymnastics that can only occur when your brain is challenged by the complexity of the tongue twister.

"I hated every minute of training, but I said, 'Don't quit. Suffer now and live the rest of your life as a champion.'"
—Muhammad Ali

WORK HARD TO MAKE IT EASY

People often ask me, "Rodney, why do you believe in tongue twisters?" The answer is simple. If I work *hard* to read the difficult tongue twister and I accomplish that goal, then reading copy is *easy*. This goes for everything that I do in voiceover and in life. If you put in the work, it will pay off. The time for relaxation and enjoying the fruits of your labor manifest after you have done your due diligence.

> "Embrace each challenge in your life as an opportunity for self-transformation."
> —Bernie S. Siegel, MD

DON'T LIMIT YOUR CHALLENGES— CHALLENGE YOUR LIMITS

It would be easy to read this book and then only practice the easy tongue twisters. If that's what you choose to do, okay. But if you really want to improve, you need to challenge yourself by mastering the hardest tongue twisters and exercises in this book.

Don't limit your degree of difficulty. Go for more difficulty and make what was once hard easy. Remember, honing your voiceover (VO) skills is the key to success.

Practicing tongue twisters in a competitive manner with a friendly rival can help you become better. Exceed your potential in general with the insertion of competition. If you don't have anyone available for such a challenge, look for someone via social media. Put the word out that you are looking for a friendly competition reading challenging tongue twisters. You will have to network to find like-minded people who are success-oriented just like you. Competition makes you push yourself harder.

THE OLD TONGUE TWISTER MODEL

Ask any voiceover actor to speak a tongue twister they know by heart and have used over and over again through the years, and they will probably repeat one of the following:

Lips teeth tip of the tongue,
Lips teeth tip of the tongue.
Lips teeth tip of the tongue.

Red letter yellow leather.
Red letter yellow leather.
Red letter yellow leather.

Those are both very good and easy to remember. You're probably also familiar with "Sally sells seashells by the seashore," "A skunk sat on a stump," and, of course, "Peter Piper." All of these famous twisters are a part of the old tongue twister model that served one purpose, and that was to trip you up as you tried to say the words rapidly and without stumbling.

THE NEW TONGUE TWISTER MODEL

The new tongue twister model is genre-specific. Do you have problems with certain phrases or consecutive letters of two and three at the beginning or end of a sentence? Is it hard for you to make your L's clear in words like *hold* or *bold*?

The new tongue twister model creates tongue twisters that help with specific problems. These twisters are not just a fun way to pass the time anymore. In this book and in the business in general, tongue twisters are a major tool for voice-over actors around the world.

Remember, when you practice tongue twisters, it's important to not just go through the motions and mumble through them. Really focus on your articulation.

Taking time to practice your pronunciation through tongue twisters is vital if you are to reach your goal of being a voice-over artist with clarity and dexterity in your speech. You have to be patient. This process takes time, but your hard work will definitely pay off in the long run.

For instance, tongue twisters help you with difficulties in pronouncing some vowel and consonant combinations, like *th*, *ea*, and *sh*. Here's a tailor-made tongue twister for you if the th sound is a problem for you. Repeat the following italicized sentence three times in a row. (Remember, your tongue goes between your teeth.)

Thirty-three thumb throbbing thick throttle thinkers thought the thirsty throttle thumper threw the throw.

Tongue twisters are a challenging and fun way to practice pronunciation and increase the clarity of your speech. Many stage actors, speakers and voiceover artists will tell you how important it is to warm up your lips, tongue, and jaw by practicing tricky twisters.

PRACTICE EVERY DAY

You should spend at least five to ten minutes practicing tongue twisters every day—and definitely that long before an audition or session. Start each new tongue twister at a slow pace. After you are comfortable with saying the words slowly, you should gradually aim for increased speed, but never at the expense of clarity. Always make sure you read exactly what is on the page. If you get in the habit of reading exactly what is on the page of tongue twisters, you will bring that same discipline to your speech and voiceover copy.

TONGUE TWISTERS ARE HARDER FOR SOME PEOPLE

Why do some people struggle with tongue twisters more than others? People see the idea of training and warming up differently. Some people don't work out at the gym or take a brisk walk a couple of times a week. Chances are, if they don't work out their bodies they would not see the value in working out or warming up their voices either.

Tongue twisters require a strong attention span along with an ability to comprehend material in short bursts while keeping a rhythmic pulse at the same time.

While it is true that you need to concentrate and that a good sense of rhythm is necessary, the benefits of doing these vocal exercises far outweigh the inherent challenges. These exercises will make you a much better reader of voiceover copy; provide you with more stamina for long-form narration, audiobooks, and video game sessions; more flexibility with your mouth; more flexibility with your tongue; and a better ability to read difficult narration, medical, and fast tag copy.

FIVE RULES TO LIVE BY

Tongue twisters don't have to be scary or overly difficult. Here are five easy-to-follow techniques you can follow to be better at reading them:

1. **Break it down**. Scan the copy and look for the most challenging parts of the tongue twister. Read it through slowly until you master it at a slow speed. Gradually get to a point where you can read the words with a good rhythmic pace.

2. **Diversify your volume**. Change your volume on each read. Start with a stage whisper. Then read at a normal level. Then project more. Then shout out the last read. These are all levels you may have to speak at when you read pieces of voiceover and speech copy.

3. **Do facial exercises**. It is important to stretch your facial muscles to loosen up and prepare to read a tongue twister. Exercising your face before and after you do tongue twisters is just like exercising your body. By regularly exercising your facial muscles, you ensure that you remain ready for fast tag copy, medical copy, and physically challenging video game copy.

4. **Write the tongue twister down.** Take the time to write the tongue twister down a few times to familiarize yourself with it.

5. **Mum's the word.** Look at the tongue twister. Read it as many times as needed silently to yourself before you utter a word aloud. The silent read is always the read that leads to the most retention. After a number of silent reads you will be much better when you read aloud.

CHAPTER **2**

Popular YouTube Twisters

Here are some of my most popular tongue twisters. You can go to YouTube and do these with me. Read all of the tongue twisters at a good pace but remember that clarity and pronunciation are always most important.

Bipidy Bumpidy

Bipidy bumpidy ripidy rumpidy
Ripidy bumpidy boo
Bipidy bumpidy ripidy rumpidy
Let's make it harder to do
Bumzidy rumzidy dumzely clumzely
Hopefully soon we'll be through
With bipidy bumpidy ripidy rumpidy
Stop when your pink tongue turns blue

The Beast in the East

The beast in the east is trying to feast
On fresh fish from French Freddy's buffet
Frowning freaking fretless weeping
For fresh salmon that fled far away
The beast in the east is trying to feast
On fried fish from San Frisco Bay
Fraught from failure to fetch from the barrel
Fresh fish from French Freddy's buffet

Why in the World

Why in the world would a whale want water?
When a whale wants water will a well run dry?
Why in the world would a wet whale want wet water?
Will a wet whale want wet water when a wet well runs dry?

Pleated Plaid Pants

Properly press the purple and black pleated plaid pants you own

Prepare to put your purple and black pleated plaid pants on

Properly press the purple and black pleated plaid pants you own

Now properly dressed in your purple and black pleated plaid pants be gone

Flame Flare

Fling flog float a flute
Flag a flirt flame flare
Flick a flack fly a flap
Flight fling flow flame flare
Flower flicker florescent flow
Flock flavor flee
Floss flagrant flash flung
Flint flake flesh flame flare

Crooked Cookies

Crooked cookies cakes and pies
Crush it crack it crapper ties
Crystal critters cry like mad
Croaking choking frogs are sad

The Pretty Banjo Player

I'm not the pretty banjo player
I'm the pretty banjo player's mate
I am only playing the pretty banjo player's banjo
'Cause the pretty banjo players running pretty late

A Simple Something

Someone said something simple
A simple something said to me
Simply simple someone said
A simple something said to me

How well did you read those tongue twisters? Did you read them clearly and with a good pace? Now, let's do them in sequence with a building tempo. The reason we do this is because when you read copy, sometimes you are required to go faster and slower for interpretation reasons. Variation in tempo makes the copy more interesting.

Notice that the instruction is written in **boldface italics**. You should only speak the words in plain text aloud.

Let's get started ...
    Bipidy bumpidy ripidy rumpidy
    Ripidy bumpidy boo
    Bipidy bumpidy ripidy rumpidy
    Let's make it harder to do
    Bumzidy rumzidy dumzely clumzely
    Hopefully soon we'll be through
    With bipidy bumpidy ripidy rumpidy
    Stop when your pink tongue turns blue

A little faster ...
    Bipidy bumpidy ripidy rumpidy
    Ripidy bumpidy boo
    Bipidy bumpidy ripidy rumpidy
    Let's make it harder to do
    Bumzidy rumzidy dumzely clumzely
    Hopefully soon we'll be through
    With bipidy bumpidy ripidy rumpidy
    Stop when your pink tongue turns blue

Is your tongue blue yet? Now, let's try a shorter one.
    Fifth smith width and worth
    Birth fourth fifth and girth
    Booth tenth tooth and truth
    Growth sleuth garth and ruth

And even faster ...
    Fifth smith width and worth
    Birth fourth fifth and girth
    Booth tenth tooth and truth
    Growth sleuth garth and ruth

That wasn't so bad, was it? This next one is something that we should all do at the end of a great meal at our favorite restaurant, especially if the service was good. Are you a big tipper? Okay, here we go ... Let's start out slow.
    Taste test the tepid tea
    Tea taste tepid warm to thee
    Tip the waiter two times three
    Two times three times four times ten
    Go right back and tip again

Now read this really fast and in one breath ...
    Taste test the tepid tea
    Tea taste tepid warm to thee
    Tip the waiter two times three
    Two times three times four times ten
    Go right back and tip again

That wasn't so bad, was it? The next tongue twister is for a more advanced voiceover actor. Beginners can read this copy, but start out slow until you feel comfortable with faster reads.

> The beast in the east is trying to feast
> On fresh fish from French freddy's buffet
> Frowning freaking fretless weeping
> For fresh salmon that fled far away
> The beast in the east is trying to feast
> On fried fish from San Frisco Bay
> Fraught from failure to fetch from the barrel
> Fresh fish from French freddy's buffet

A little faster ...

> The beast in the east is trying to feast
> On fresh fish from French freddy's buffet
> Frowning freaking fretless weeping
> For fresh salmon that fled far away
> The beast in the east is trying to feast
> On fried fish from San Frisco Bay
> Fraught from failure to fetch from the barrel
> Fresh fish from French freddy's buffet

Now let's try it really fast!
    The beast in the east is trying to feast
    On fresh fish from French Freddy's buffet
    Frowning freaking fretless weeping
    For fresh salmon that fled far away
    The beast in the east is trying to feast
    On fried fish from San Frisco Bay
    Fraught from failure to fetch from the barrel
    Fresh fish from French Freddy's buffet

Very good!

CHAPTER **3**

Warm-Ups Before and During a Session

BE SURE TO YAWN BEFORE YOU START ANY VOCAL exercise. Yawning relaxes the body, opens the mouth, and prepares you for speaking. This is not difficult and it shouldn't be if it is something you are going to do before or within a session. Realize, it is important to save your energy, both physically and mentally, to read long-form copy.

"Sometimes when you are in a long session, like for an audiobook, you can take short breaks and do a series of vocal warm-ups that serve to keep you loose and sharp for the next words in the copy that you have to read. These short sentences

---

Working hard leaves enough time to rest, but hardworking people still use these resting moments to work."

—Terry Mark

cover all of the vowels in the English language that are surely to be used in the copy you are reading.

If you get a break during the session, and certainly before you start, go through the following exercise designed to keep you loose and open you up vocally.

Repeat the vowels 3 times in a row.
 A E I O U
 A E I O U
 A E I O U

Now, stretch it out with these color names that start with the vowels.

Amber Evergreen Indigo Olive Ultraviolet and sometimes Y

Amber Evergreen Indigo Olive Ultraviolet and sometimes Y

Amber Evergreen Indigo Olive Ultraviolet and sometimes Y

Repeat this exercise as many times as you want or have time for and get back to your session. Remember, doing tongue twisters and vocal exercises is equivalent to a professional basketball team warming up before the game.

SENSE MEMORY

Proper placement of the tongue is one of the most important aspects of reading voiceover copy. This is not something that you should think about while reading copy, but if you work on proper placement while practicing tongue twisters, you will do it habitually correctly when you are working. Proper placement of the tongue can cure the worst of speech impediments, mouth clicks, and chronic diction problems (see chapter 7).

Following is an exercise called "sense memory" that is commonly used by stage actors. With sense memory, you are not concerned immediately with what comes out of our mouth audibly but more about what it *feels* like when you say the words that come out of your mouth. When you place your tongue correctly behind your teeth or on the roof of your mouth or suspended in air in the middle of your mouth to produce the desired pronunciation and sound, your sense memory remembers the proper position that your tongue was in when you were perfect in your pronunciation. That is using your sense memory while doing tongue twisters.

"Memory is the diary that we carry about with us."
—Oscar Wilde

SENSE MEMORY EXERCISES

When you say **oh** the tongue should be suspended in the middle of your mouth.

When you say **eh** the tongue should be suspended in the lower middle of your mouth.

When you say **the** or any other word that begins with **th**, your tongue is in between your bottom and top front teeth.

When you say **luck** or any word that begins with an **L**, your tongue should be up against the roof of your mouth.

Whenever you have a word that is giving you trouble, remember how it feels when you do say it correctly and recall that feeling in your mouth and outside of your mouth. How did your lips feel? How did your jaws feel? You need to remember where your tongue was placed when you reached your desired pronunciation and never forget it. That is using your sense memory.

"One way to break up any kind of tension is good deep breathing."
—Byron Nelson, pro golfer

DEEP BREATHING

Let's talk about breathing. You are definitely going to need good breathing technique to properly work through this book as well as all of the voiceover copy you read every day. My method of proper breathing is based on what I learned as a voice major at the University of Michigan's School of Music. I will explain breathing to you in the simplest form, as it was taught to me.

LEARN HOW TO BREATHE PROPERLY

Stand up. Draw air in slowly through your nose. Your belly should fill up like a balloon while your chest remains stationary. Fill up as much as you can and then release it as slowly as you took it in. You should pull your stomach muscles in as you exhale, as if you were sucking in your gut to pose for a photograph. Repeat this several times until it starts to become second nature.

Now, place the palm of your hand on your stomach and prepare to add a sound to your exhale. Add the *ahhhh* sound to your exhale and do it in one breath for as long as you can. Again, repeat this process over and over until it starts to become second nature.

It may seem exaggerated and awkward at first, but pretty soon it will become habitual and you will do it naturally whenever you speak.

To make it easy for the air to escape from you properly, as you speak, your mouth should be open wide and your throat should be relaxed. Your diaphragm is like an air pump and you want to reduce the resistance the air experiences; so try to be really relaxed when you vocalize with the *ahhhh* sound.

The voice should be placed in the mask which is your face. You should feel a resonance or vibration in your forehead and the bridge of your nose if the placement of your voice is correct. Proper placement takes the strain off of your vocal cords.

Okay, you started with the *ahhhh* sound while practicing your breathing pattern. Now, let's add some tongue-twisting words to the process.

Inhale deeply but stay relaxed without tension as you repeat these words as many times as you can in one breath.

Flip Flapping
Flipping and flapping
Wishing and wanting
Dipping and dumping
Picking and popping
Fatty batty titter tatty
Sloppy floppy choppy hobby
Tick tacky tickle tackle
Super duper tricky saddle

Now that you've mastered basic breathing techniques, let's put your new technique to use when you read fast tags.

"If a tongue twister's tongue could twist, how many twists would the tongue twister's tongue twist while their tongue was a twisting?"
—G.K. Griswold

CHAPTER **4**

Fast Tags

A TAG IS READ BY THE ANNOUNCER OF THE SPOT OR A different person. Sometimes, and especially after a commercial, tags have to be read fast, which can be a problem if you don't know the proper technique to read the copy in the allotted time.

First, let's define *tag*. Tags are:

- ❏ Information placed at the end of a *commercial* that may include a date, time, phone number, and website address.
- ❏ Information after a *promo* that may include an air date
- ❏ Information after a *trailer* that may include a legal disclaimer, a movie rating, and screening locations.

Let's go over a few techniques that will help you read tags faster.

USE ONE BREATH

It is generally better to read as much of the copy as you can in one breath. It is not mandatory however, as long as you maintain the same tempo for the duration of the tag. That way, the engineer can take the breath out and put the tag together without adjusting the tempo of either line.

LITTLE OR NO MELODY

Fast tags are generally read with little melody. In other words, there should be no constant up and down in your phrasing. Melody and going up and down on words and sentences like a roller coaster takes time and energy. A flat monotone read without a lot of melody or peaks and valleys will give you the energy and wind to finish paragraphs in one breath.

READ IN BLOCKS

Focus on blocks of words at a time rather than the standard one-word-at-a-time method. View a sentence as a whole and try to comprehend the meaning of the words as a group.

See the next line long before you speak it. Avoid subvocalization habits (pronouncing each word in your head as you read it). Don't think, just read. Thinking too much can slow down your speed.

Don't be concerned about what you might have missed, don't self-direct while you are reading. The director and the engineer are listening for words that you missed. If you screwed up a few words, they will just ask you to do it over or do a pick-up and fix the words you missed.

PRACTICE

When you read fast tags you should be on automatic pilot. Take a good look at the script before you read it and familiarize yourself with it. Practice it at top speed. When you read the copy during the session, your goal is to read the entire piece as clear and as fast as you can.

When you practice you need to get rid of distractions. You can probably increase your speed if you reduce distractions to a bare minimum. Find a solitary place to read fast tags, and turn off the TV, radio, and cell phone.

SAMPLE FAST TAGS

Disclaimer: *In order to simulate the type of copy you will encounter in the real world, I wrote all of the sample tags in this chapter using the names of real manufacturers and products. I do not, however, claim to represent any of the manufacturers or products that are mentioned.*

Safety

Because safety is a priority the time quoted is not a guarantee just an estimate. It may take longer. You must ask for this limited time offer. Prices, participation, delivery area and charges may vary. Minimum order per delivery no double portions. Ordering available to 2:00 PM. Tax and delivery charge extra. See menu for more details.

Ratings

Rated-PG 13. Some material may be inappropriate for children under 13. Now playing in theaters everywhere.

Rated PG. Parental guidance suggested. Some material may not be suitable for children.

Offer Good

Offer good at participating stores through July 11 Trade-in phone restrictions apply. All trade-ins final. Not available where prohibited by law.

Carryout

Johnny Bee's carryout only. Side dishes may be extra. You must ask for this limited time offer. Prices, participation, delivery area, and charges may vary. Johnny Bee's is a registered trademark of Johnny Bee's IP holder LLC.

Plush Mobil

The Silver Mirror Ball Lamp with Laser Design shade for $19.99 and the Virtual Space Lamp for $39.99 are a limited time offer. Other new Blacklight responsive products include Plush Mobiles at $12.99 and Glow Starblast $14.99. Rainbow Jumbo Gift Sets both at $19.99 are not returnable items based on the registered trademark of plush Mobile textile and digital industries IP holder LLC.

Lenscrafters

Lenscrafter's best $99 offer is a one-time promotional offer. To get a complete pair of glasses with Dura Lens you must qualify for this limited offer by submitting an optometrist-written prescription along with a receipt proving purchase of said items aforementioned in the copy previously read. Scratchproof plastic lens for only $99 available only at the $99 Dura Lens event. Restrictions apply. Must be a resident of the United States to participate in this optical event. Seasonal changes applicable must show proof of citizenship to apply.

Honda

Honda's two-point-two-percent financing only applies on the second Tuesday of each month. All dealer markdowns apply on all other days of the week except Sunday. All other cars on the lot will be sold at maximum profit as determined by the salesperson at the time of sale. Certain conditions apply. Offer good for those with approved credit.

FAST LEGAL TAGS

As I said before, it is important to practice reading fast tags in sequence with a building tempo. The reason to do this is because when you read copy, sometimes you are required to go faster and slower for interpretation reasons. Variation in tempo makes the copy more interesting.

It is important to practice reading tags every day. Here are a few exercises that will help you improve your legal tag reading speed. Remember, articulation and clarity is critical.

The instruction is written in **_boldface italics_**. You should only speak the words in plain text aloud.

Let's start out slowly.

Johnny Bee's carryout only. Side dishes may be extra. You must ask for this limited time offer. Prices, participation, delivery area, and charges may vary. Johnny Bee's is a registered trademark of Johnny Bee's IP holder LLC.

A little faster ...

Johnny Bee's carryout only. Side dishes may be extra. You must ask for this limited time offer. Prices, participation, delivery area, and charges may vary. Johnny Bee's is a registered trademark of Johnny Bee's IP holder LLC.

And now, really fast and in one breath ...

Johnny Bee's carryout only. Side dishes may be extra. You must ask for this limited time offer. Prices, participation, delivery area, and charges may vary. Johnny Bee's is a registered trademark of Johnny Bee's IP holder LLC.

And even faster ...

Johnny Bee's carryout only. Side dishes may be extra. You must ask for this limited time offer. Prices, participation, delivery area, and charges may vary. Johnny Bee's is a registered trademark of Johnny Bee's IP holder LLC.

You don't have to be fast, but you must be quick. If you can do it in one breath, that's great—but you don't have to. Be quick within every line and you will be faster overall.

Let's start this next one out slowly.

Offer good at participating stores through July 11. Trade-in phone restrictions apply. All trade-ins final. Not available where prohibited by law.

A little faster ...

Offer good at participating stores through July 11. Trade-in phone restrictions apply. All trade-ins final. Not available where prohibited by law.

And even faster ...

Offer good at participating stores through July 11. Trade-in phone restrictions apply. All trade-ins final. Not available where prohibited by law.

Very good! The next tag is for a more-advanced voice-over actor. Beginners can also read this copy, but start out slow until you feel comfortable with faster reads.

Because safety is a priority the time quoted is not a guarantee just an estimate. It may take longer. You must ask for this limited time offer. Prices, participation, delivery area, and charges may vary. Minimum order per delivery no double portions. Offer available to 2:00 PM. Tax and delivery charge extra. See menu for more details.

A little faster ...

Because safety is a priority the time quoted is not a guarantee just an estimate. It may take longer. You must ask for this limited time offer. Prices, participation, delivery area, and charges may vary. Minimum order per delivery no double portions. Offer available to 2:00 PM. Tax and delivery charge extra. See menu for more details.

And now, really fast and in one breath ...

Because safety is a priority the time quoted is not a guarantee just an estimate. It may take longer. You must ask for this limited time offer. Prices, participation, delivery area, and charges may vary. Minimum order per delivery no double portions. Offer available to 2:00 PM. Tax and delivery charge extra. See menu for more details.

Very good!

CHAPTER **5**

Movie Trailer Legal Tags

IN THIS CHAPTER, WE ARE GOING TO READ MOVIE TRAILER legal tags in sequence. Again, notice that the instruction is written in ***boldface italics***. You should only speak the words in plain text aloud.

"Let's start out slowly.

Rating PG. Parental Guidance suggested. Some material may not be suitable for children. Now playing in theaters everywhere.

A little faster ...

Rating PG. Parental Guidance suggested. Some material may not be suitable for children. Now playing in theaters everywhere.

And even faster ...

Rating PG. Parental Guidance suggested. Some material may not be suitable for children. Now playing in theaters everywhere.

Let's switch it up a little.

Rated-PG 13. Some material may be inappropriate for children under 13. Now playing in theaters everywhere.

A little faster ...

Rated-PG 13. Some material may be inappropriate for children under 13. Now playing in theaters everywhere.

Words speak to me, the scripts speak to me. I've always been enchanted with the language. I think it's a wonderful thing."
—Don LaFontaine

CHAPTER **6**

Spoken Word TongueTwisters

To my knowledge, I am the first to design a group of spoken word tongue twisters. I have long been a fan of spoken word poetry, a performance-based art form that focuses on word play and storytelling. I decided to use this way of speaking to prepare for reading long narration and specifically audiobook narration. I found that when I constructed long sentences with a little rhyme, slang, repetition, and challenging words, it was a great source of warm-up and preparation for long and tedious sessions.

Read the following copy as if you were standing onstage in a dimly lit small café at a spoken word poetry event. Rhythm is very important when you read these tongue twisters. Be more aggressive and "in your face" than you are with the other tongue twisters.

These twisters don't make much sense. I wrote whatever came to mind at the time and I didn't edit or rewrite any of these selections. Everything here is raw and exactly what I was thinking at that time in my life.

Have fun with it. There is no punctuation. You make your own commas, periods, etc. And remember, you should be more concerned about articulation and exactly what is on the page. No adlibbing please.

These should be read at a good pace. Enunciation is very important. Don't mumble. Speak clearly and distinctly.

Use facial expressions. Smile if you're reading something happy. Did you know that you can literally hear a smile? Don't smile if you are reading something serious. Use the appropriate facial expressions and gestures for the various emotions expressed in this spoken word tongue twister copy.

"Spoken word tongue twisters mentally stimulate."
–Rodney Saulsberry

NONSENSE

An accent is easy to accept as long as it is accessed accurately ascending in ascension to esthetics ethics and essential essence irrevocable irreconcilable indescribably indelibly delectable and irascibly contrived to the point of incredulous simultaneous combustion at the risk of salutations that rise above the lifeless lineless numbness of the vernacular that holds us all captive to the serene calm of prism hypnotism and paradigm-driven resistance to the futuristic realm of the charismatic adventures of the poets and scholars that wander the halls of prestigious universities around the globe. Libation is in order if you need a drink knowledge is in order if you want to think the case is driven by witnesses whose stories change every day lost on the road is your navigation okay are you precise in a world that thrives on delay put off to tomorrow what you could do today tomorrow next week or maybe not at all no longer obsessed with how tall or how small didn't know about the latest technology didn't know about the winner of the spelling bee I'm still rejoicing about the men on the moon but maybe we went there too soon.

CALL BACK

From the pillars of success to a pit of deception a commitment to someone who wishes you good riddance but you choose to stay to fight for your way and long for the day that they hear what you say try a more bitter taste hey give a case of the midnight blues do you stand accused of delivering a fuse to light the park keep us out of the dark run walk or fly to never try would be a travesty a place where butterflies dare to be free from everyday chatter and reckless matter of facts in a row both crooked and straight you got up early and yet you were still late for the ball for the walk down the hall to the house of pain hard work more gain stop doing different and singing the same tune it up drink a cup of mint or lint all over your clothes a turtleneck short-sleeve apple cider fill the clouds with petty cash beef steak turkey and balderdash football baseball a click and a clack a summer winter share a splinter vow wow how now brown cow later trait gate and a poodle of a dog a farm and a hog a water creek and a bump on the log London fog don't like the smog never let a tongue twister call you Bob or Betty or Benny nor Sue it's me no it's you everlasting battery and tobacco chew a million bites are afraid of heights blinded by the city lights under pressure the bedroom dresser the clock on the wall is striking out like a rugby player who never found how maybe a call to your brother could change your life pursue the opera what a night to get the news that lost and found is visceral elliptical politically correct bound by law to obey and respect I'll be right back almost checklist driven frostbite cold sometimes I tell the story about the alley cat when your teeth get cold you should wear a hat a scarf exactly a reason to repeat after me I will always be studying to be the best that I can be a quiet thinker fascinated by words the expressions confessions magnificent bug repellant registered voter kite floater I will give you the world if you promise to give it back I will give you more tongue twisters silent critters beans and fritters and a promise to call you back.

BUSY

Don't get yourself in a tizzy just because you find yourself always in a state of busy doing all that matters to get you to the place where life is better for you and the animals at the local zoo and all that glitters is not gold when life itself is two-fold three-fold with pie à la mode giving you weight and tight fitting clothes that fluctuate with each piece of cake words and scores if attitude projected at you and your sisters new dude who came from the place of interlude so bright is the day that proceeds the night the sound of the cockpit as we take flight you know the pilot is a traffic controller now that you graduated they feel more bolder I pity the person who can't cry on a shoulder a loose-leaf folder a number two pencil and inkjet smolder of fire can we take it higher to the conception of a PF Flyer a Nike Cross Trainer or an All Star prior to the law he broke climb high up the tree without no fear tell your loved one I love you dear John the letter started and now they are departed can I intertwine the time line and pay a fine for drinking red wine or is somewhere over the rainbow that my dogs barked and my cat meowed and a girl named Sue bought a fishing rod or an Easter bunny on the fourth of July I cherish the sun and the winter sleigh ride the turkey based and a sweet potato pie bang a drum in total sum I add the sugar to the drink and stare ahead as I try to never ever blink caption traction I'm just trying to get a reaction some satisfaction some rest from the complications of this tongue twisting mess.

BE

Faced with the problem of what to do next perplexed in indecision inquisition and biography telepathy apartment hunting furnish a room sweep the floor with a nylon broom speak on a panel no act on TV stretched out in too many directions oh no woe is me who said that we can't do more than one thing at a time stop on a dime and drink Malbec red wine from Argentina oh it's good only one glass at a business function did you ever watch petticoat junction or Mr. Ed or did you watch the Flintstones and Yogi Bear instead? never was good at baseball hall of fame Pete Rose gambled what a shame will Mayweather ever fight Manny Pacquiao will singers stop the opera and never bow again or never before close the door on magic capers strange universe and comedy shakers wrinkled suits stuffed in a suitcase never cheat in a marathon race never tell a secret and fall from grace I can taste the sugar in a grape a sour piece of candy can spoil a date did you go with the intentions of being sedate or wide awake in a rage of faith to follow the preacher the grade school teacher the professor who taught you what ten times eight times five would be if you could see past infinity it's never too late to learn to be a hipster be a person who can master any tongue twister no matter how fast you read it say it or shout it be all about it commit to the task at hand and be the best that you can be.

LIFE

They said the lease was up but it wasn't really true three more years till the date is due don't depend on others to provide for you last week after the show hooked up to dialysis paralysis prenuptial analysis Mandalay excursion to a faraway land Spanish is the brand matriculate postulate early turn dark when it's not even late impaired glaucoma no not me make all your doctor visits so you can see every chart my heart education proclamation democratic population seismic surgical suture sitter dentures drastic diversity stickers in the way we pontificate demonstrate and isolate repossession first half stats reflect relevance benevolence take a chance on hats a derby a fedora a skullcap and more didn't you tell them you were opening a hat store? never mind I digress international mandatory test to determine the width of humanity on your chest Minnesota South Dakota are you up or down? are you in for the winter plan to stay on the ground or is your suitcase packed and scheduled to fly send her money no return raked the leaves let them burn notice all the wrinkles in the road at the turn at the wheel of public opinion visit jeep dot com not even close want a cookie? I really don't want to play to the beat of a gospel hymn and a leading voice with a message to spread go to bed and wake up fresh as a daisy mae if you are truly needy step up to the plate ask for a donate but you are too proud to beg Fred shame on you sleepy black and aqua blue benched oppositions tongue twisting decisions I refuse to bend I will never call it the end because I can handle the seamier steamier strain and strife simply because it's life.

STOCKS

Give me the reason to buy a stock a blue chip IPO pop stock a stock that can rise to the top of the pop charts a popular perennial preferred stock not your penny stock stock from the broker at the pawn shop or an oversold silicon valley tech stock I want a rise to the top unheard of stock a knick knack patty wack give your dog a bone stock plop my money down on the phone with Dow Jones stock feel swell at the opening bell stock not a bell-weathered tar and feathered foreign stock from Wales stock I want to read the ticker tape vacillate contemplate lose my hair buy more shares can't sleep at night too excited to care kind of stock frenzy Benzy Jag and a Cadillac two-story mansion oh yes give me that not the split not the splat not the conservative bid not the secure serene safe stock with a bid lid give me the sky is the limit stratospheric inordinate amount of stock the aggressive excessive unrestrained leaps and bounds like a bunny no like a kangaroo hop stock the extravagant immoderate and unreasonable buy give me one zillion shares and let me fly!

Congratulations! You have completed Section I. I am really proud of you. In review, you have gone over some tough tongue twisters, fast tags, breathing exercises, and spoken word tongue twisters that should have gotten you warmed up and prepared for the challenging road ahead. Don't let this be the last time that you visit the preceding pages. Refer to them often to help clarify upcoming text and concepts.

Switching gears, we will next discuss some of the challenges we face every day in voiceover when it comes to recording.

Section 2

Voiceover Challenges

"Obstacles are those frightful things you see when you take your eyes off the goal."
–HENRY FORD

CHAPTER **7**

Mouth Noises and Other Issues

I LOVE TONGUE TWISTERS BECAUSE THEY GIVE ME A CHANCE to speak freely without worry. I often use them to practice ways to avoid problems when I read voiceover copy. For example, if I want to practice avoiding mouth noises, plosive words, and sibilance, I can experiment and test different solutions saying tongue twisters in the microphone.

In this chapter, a few of my colleagues and I are going to share our methods of dealing with mouth clicks, plosive words, and sibilance. The bottom line is: if you take the time to experiment with ways to avoid and limit the challenges, you will prevail.

Disclaimer: *I am not a professional recording engineer, and neither are any of the other voiceover professionals who generously contributed to this chapter. Any advice about the technical aspects of recording equipment offered in this section should be considered purely anecdotal. In other words, we are simply sharing with you what works for us. Please consult a professional recording engineer before using your equipment or before making any changes to your home studio setup.*

"Efficiency is doing things right.
Effectiveness is doing the right things."
—Peter Drucker

MOUTH NOISES/CLICKS

There is one point I want to address right off the bat: pop filters do not prevent mouth noises, they only mask them to a certain extent. You will probably always record some mouth noise, it just comes with the territory. It is unavoidable.

Most clicks occur from your lips when you open and close your mouth. Please, don't make this a constant worry or even a slight concern when you are recording. Your mind should be on your performance.

Water is always the great remedy—for everything. A dry mouth definitely leads to more mouth clicks. A water-fed mouth leads to good hydration and less mouth clicks.

On the other hand, it is important to note that not all irritating sounds emanate from the mouth cavity. There are also those nagging, bubbling sounds that emanate from your stomach. Yes, the microphone will pick those up too. Of course, you can adjust the microphone in a way to lessen it from picking up stomach sounds, but it would perhaps be best to avoid carbonated drinks before a session.

The good news is that most mouth clicks usually happen in the clear when you are not actually speaking, which makes them a lot easier to delete in post-session.

I have said it before and I will say it again: Please do not be obsessed with mouth noises, stomach noises, and sibilance. You can destroy the essence of a performance if you sanitize the initial delivery to a fault. If you take the time to listen to some of the recordings from the 1940s and 50s that your parents used to play on those turntables, you will hear a ton of mouth clicks, breaths, and sibilance, along with some fantastic performances!

> "I never teach my pupils. I only attempt to provide the conditions in which they can learn."
> —Albert Einstein

Mike Elmore, Voice Actor

It's well known in the community that green apples are a great remedy for mouth noise. I personally take three bites and then chase it all with a gulp of room-temperature water when I am hearing these unwanted sounds. I'm good for about ten minutes after that.

As far as the plosives/puffs of air in the recording ... of course, using a pop filter is mandatory, but sometimes that is not enough. The best thing to do is learn to control the amount of air you produce on these P's, D's, T's, and B's. In the meantime, and in addition to this, you can angle the pop filter slightly. Bring the bottom of it a little closer to your chin area, tilting the top more toward the mic. Trying varying degrees of this will yield good results in deflecting the puffs of air even more than it would in a "normal," vertical position.

Trever Altabef, Voice Actor

Whenever the issue about mouth clicks comes up it drives me crazy because there is no remedy. Water only makes your mouth more moist, which produces more clicks. In my opinion, it's all about the tongue. If you have good articulation and enunciation (which is basically the same thing), your tongue will be in the right place in your mouth which should lessen the mouth noise. I make a special effort to warm-up properly with exercises that challenge my tongue before I read copy.

DRY MOUTH

If you are experiencing a case of dry mouth, take a sip of room-temperature water and swirl it around in your mouth before you swallow it. Now, do the tongue twister below at the tempo of a ticking clock. Do this as many times as is necessary until you feel hydrated and ready to read your copy.

Moist Mouth

Moist mouth moist mouth moist mouth tic toc
Moist mouth moist mouth moist mouth tick toc
Moist mouth moist mouth moist mouth tick toc

Still feeling a little dry? Take another sip and read the following tongue twister.

Cure the Thirst

Coat the throat with a water burst
Take two sips to cure the thirst
No more smacking no voice cracking
No dry lips and "P" pop tracking
Pick ups and pop ups and plosives and plurals
Sibilance ambivalence in a desert dry world
What do you do to stop the curse?
Coat the throat with a water burst
Take two sips to cure the thirst

"People still think of me as a cartoonist, but the only thing I lift a pen or pencil for these days is to sign a contract, a check, or an autograph."
—Walt Disney

THE PLOSIVE "P"

If you are working in close proximity of the microphone and you have to use a word with a plosive P just put a pencil on your lips. It splits the sound instead of the full blast going into the microphone. Although, I have never used this technique, it is something that other voiceover artists have used in animation and video-game sessions.

"The single biggest problem in communication is the illusion that it has taken place."
–George Bernard Shaw

DO YOU REALLY HAVE A SIBILANCE ISSUE?

If you believe that you have a sibilance problem, the cure truly starts with you abandoning the acceptance of your so-called sibilance problem. I believe that is the true beginning of not having the problem anymore!

Here are some tips for controlling vocal sibilance. Firstly, you have to learn to trust your instincts, ears, and common sense. When you are working in a session, the engineers will let you know if you are having sibilance issues. They will remedy the situation by switching the microphone, instructing you to stand farther back from the microphone, or by fixing the problem post session.

Here is what I do at the microphone to avoid all potential problems. I step up to the microphone with complete confidence that I am going to accomplish what I am trying to do with great success. I take a sip of room-temperature water and swirl it around in my mouth. Just this sip of water alone will help me avoid mouth clicks, sibilance, and overall dry-mouth issues. I stand at a distance from the microphone that is sure to pick up my projected voice, but not every nonverbal nuance and utterance that comes out of my body.

The microphone even better serves a person with a noticeable lisp if they stand in the right place in terms of distance from the mic. When I am at home in my studio, recording myself, I also try to maintain that positive attitude. So, if my head is right and I am not looking for trouble, when I prepare my MP3 presentation to be sent off to my agent or client, I don't destroy the integrity of the audition by editing out all of the natural sounds that come from the human voice. I don't take the breaths out to a fault and I don't run it through any type of processor to compensate for sibilance.

My first and usually most successful approach to avoid sibilance, plosives, and mouth clicks is to make sure I use proper technique. Please, don't get me wrong—I will use some of the aids on the market, like a pop filter and popper stopper—but at the end of the day, it is still up to me to execute in a manner where no external forces are needed to help me prevent failure and to accomplish success.

These simple mic techniques should help you with sibilance:
1. Settle on a good distance from the microphone that prevents popping.

2. Move in close to the microphone when you want to speak more quietly.
3. Work off axis when close to the left or the right to avoid popping.
4. Back away from the microphone when you are shouting.

Additionally, try this exercise:

A Sibilance Tongue Twister

Stop right now
Stop stressing those S's
Stop making sipping sounds
With super-sonic sentences
Sip some water sip some tea
And simply take a stance
Change your microphone position
And no more sibilance

Record the preceding tongue twister while getting really close to your microphone. Then listen to the playback and notice how apparent the S's are. Next, record the tongue twister standing about a foot and a half from the mic. Then listen to the playback with a positive ear that is not looking for a sibilance problem. Do you truly have a sibilance problem or are you just too close to the microphone?

SIBILANCE REVIEW

- Stand far enough away from the microphone to avoid plosives.
- Stand far enough away from the microphone to avoid sibilance.
- Speak off axis to the right or left of the microphone when you move in closer.
- Drink room-temperature water to avoid a dry mouth.
- Avoid things like dairy or caffeine before and during a session.

I have come to embrace the use of pop filters and popper stoppers; and consider them valuable assets to making my sessions successful.

Using the proper technique and distance, practice recording these sentences on mic without sibilance problems during playback.

Silly Sibilance Sentences

Silly senseless sibilance sentences
Separate seagulls from southern semblances
Serious decisions several musicians
Sanctioned songs for soprano mistresses
Supersonic sensitive fences
Suppository savory succulent pittances
Sibilance sounding sibilance causing
Silly senseless Sibilance sentences

> "Even if you are happy with the life you've chosen, you're still curious about the other options."
> —Taylor Swift

MORE OPINIONS

Even though I firmly believe using mic technique, in terms of distance from the microphone, and mic placement can significantly decrease mouth noises and sibilance, there are other opinions from industry professionals. Here are some other points of view on the subject of sibilance:

Devon Kersey, Voice Actor

I always Compress for Success! I don't have time to be concerned about proper distance or pop filters, I just use my compressor and de-esser before I send it off. I used to spend a lot of time setting the levels, but now I just push record and talk. The compressor kills the sibilance and keeps the track consistent.

Sheila Rose, Singer

I have to compress my voice because it's really high and I have a severe sibilance problem. I recently bought a Kaotica Eyeball. It really cuts down the mouth noise and the sibilance but I still have to use a de-esser.

Tonya Allan, Voice Actor

The biggest mistake newbies make is adding reverb to their voiceover auditions. That process actually brings out the sharpness and big sibilant S's. You should never put reverb on a voiceover. Keep it flat and you can avoid high-end frequencies and sibilance.

Jimmy Lestivich, Voice Actor

When I have a lot of sibilant and plosive words in a piece of copy, I tape a pencil to the front of my tube microphone. It splits the air going directly into the microphone and cuts down on the sibilance and pops, so I don't have to edit them out later.

Ulysses Yates, Voice Actor

I am very sensitive when it comes to sibilance because I have always had a problem with my S's. I was told by an engineer to stand ten to eighteen inches away from the microphone. I was also taught to aim the microphone downward and work off axis. Yet, I still have to use a de-esser when I make an MP3 to send off to my agents. I do find that the louder I listen back, the more problems I hear. I would hope that when a client receives my audition, they are not blasting it and listening to it like you would listen to rock music.

CHAPTER **8**

Blended Sounds

IT IS NOT UNUSUAL FOR SOME BLENDED SOUNDS TO BE challenging. Do you have any words with consonant combinations that are generally a challenge for you? Here are some two- and three-letter blend tongue twisters that will help you articulate words that start with blended letters. If any of these consonant combinations is a problem for you, this is a great exercise.

"A nice blend of prediction and surprise seem to be at the heart of the best art."
—Wendy Carlos

TWO-LETTER BLENDS

Blistering Blizzards

Blended bloated blinded blight
Bless blink black and blue
Blended bloated blinded blight
Blistering blizzards blew by you
Blitz blast blob and bloke
Blessed blinked bladder and bloat
Blubber blunt blissfully blue
Blistering blizzards blew by you

Snoring Snails

Snore snail snap snoop
Sneak snuck snout snoot
Snarl sneer snipe snip
Sniff snuff snake snitch
Squabble Squealers
Squirrels squash squids
Squids squeeze squats
Squawkers squint and squeal
Squealers squabble and squat

A **Twist Tweet**

Twister twit twat
Twinkle tweet truck
Twist twine twin
Twice twenty twitch

The **TR** Sound

Trickle treat tread
Tractor trunk trinket
True troop triple
Trend train tread

THREE-LETTER BLENDS

Strictly Strong

Strictly structured stretch and stride
Straight strident strong with pride
Struggle strum strike and strung
Street streak stream and strong

Three Throw

Thrust Three Threw
Through Thrive Throat
Thrice Thread Throne
Threat Throw Thrash

FOUR-LETTER BLENDS

Extravagant Expression

Extravagant extraordinary extraction
Expressive express expression
Excretion explicit explanation
Explode explosion explain

This is Not

Read the following sentence three times fast.

This is not a particularly peculiar particular predicament

This is not a particularly peculiar particular predicament

This is not a particularly peculiar particular predicament

Lunch Crunch

Lunch punch hunch crunch
Couch ouch pouch crouch
Much such crutch touch
Stench trench wrench bench
Search church perch lurch
Starch march parch arch
Fetch catch watch match
Hatch patch swatch and latch

Brash Trash

Crash splash smash
Trash flash stash
Mash brash thrash
Clash wash establish

Did any of the preceding tongue twisters address your problem with consonant blends? Obviously I could go on and on with different combinations, but I want to take this opportunity to encourage you to create your own tongue twisters based on the sounds and combinations that you find difficult.

One of the hardest words for me to say in voiceover copy is *remember*. One day, I will have to come up with a tongue twister to help me get over that obstacle.

CHAPTER **9**

Punctuation

I**T IS IMPORTANT TO FOLLOW THE PUNCTUATION MARKS IN** voiceover copy. Punctuation is used to create a sense of clarity in sentences and it will help you interpret the copy.

Below is a great exercise to help you practice paying attention to punctuation marks. Start by silently reading the copy below to yourself one time; then read it again, but this time speak aloud and actually say each punctuation aloud, including the period.

"Every day, you make thousands of choices—many of them involving, well ... risk. Things like ... what should I do on vacation? How fast can this baby go? Should I trade up to a bigger place? Risk—influences every choice you make ... and reflects what we like to call your risk appetite. But, managing risk isn't just something you do in your personal life. At

BNY Sloan Kettering, it's part of your work, too. Risk taking is a fundamental part of providing financial services. There are degrees of risk and choices to be made about how much and what types of risk we take on."

Now, read aloud the first line from the script.

"Every day, you make thousands of choices—many of them involving, well … risk."

Now, read the line aloud and also include speaking the punctuation.

"Every day COMMA you make thousands of choices DASH many of them involving COMMA well ELLIPSIS risk PERIOD"

Next, read the entire script without saying the punctuations aloud. Did you follow the punctuations throughout the entire script better this time? If you follow this ritual every time you read a new piece of copy, you will be sure to interpret the copy more closely with the copywriter's intent as you go about delivering your own interpretation. Here is a more elaborate version of the punctuation exercise.

Try to say this bit of logic quickly while making sense.

If you understand, say, "understand."

If you don't understand, say, "don't understand."

But if you understand and say, "don't understand,"

How do I understand that you understand? Understand!

Did you ask a question at the end? Try it again.

    If you understand, say, "understand."

    If you don't understand, say, "don't understand."

    But if you understand and say, "don't understand,"

    How do I understand that you understand? Understand!

Did you do it again? Take it slower and remember that there is an exclamation point at the end, not a question mark.

    If you understand, say, "understand."

    If you don't understand, say, "don't understand."

    But if you understand and say, "don't understand,"

    How do I understand that you understand? Understand!

The bottom line: you must pay attention to the punctuation in the text you read. It makes all the difference in the world.

"Punctuation is used to create a sense of clarity in sentences. You need to use the punctuation marks to help you interpret VO copy."
—Rodney Saulsberry

CHAPTER **10**

A Spanish Tongue Twister

One of the biggest challenges for English speakers (and Asians) is learning the Spanish pronunciation of R. Getting your tongue to roll takes practice!

Following are several versions of the tongue twister *Tres tristes tigres* (Three sad tigers) I found on the Internet. I guarantee reading these aloud will help you to roll your R's in Spanish. (Unfortunately, I was unable to find a satisfactory English translation.)

VERSION 1

Tres tristes tigres tragaban trigo en un trigal en tres tristes trastos. En tres tristes trastos tragaban trigo tres tristes tigres.

VERSION 2

Tres tristes tigres triscaban trigo en un trigal. Un tigre, dos tigres, tres tigres trigaban en un trigal. ¿Qué tigre trigaba más? Todos trigaban igual.

VERSION 3

En tres tristes trastos de trigo, tres tristes tigres comían trigo. Comían trigo, tres tristes tigres, en tres tristes trastos de trigo.

"Those who know nothing of foreign languages know nothing of their own."
—Johann Wolfgang von Goethe

CHAPTER **11**

Avoid "Announcer" Delivery

O NE OF THE MOST ANNOYING THINGS ABOUT READING promo voiceover copy these days is the current trend of not sounding like an announcer when the copy is obviously written for an announcer. It seems like every VO direction I read lately has directions like "not too announcery" and "non-announcerish." (If you check the dictionary, those two words don't exist.) Producers and writers of commercial copy created this form of directional slang.

"My whole philosophy is to broadcast the way a fan would broadcast."

–Harry Caray

Here are some tips on how to take the announcer read out of your promo copy:

1. Don't articulate so much
2. More legato and less staccato
3. End each line going down or level
4. Make it more conversational
5. Don't shout
6. Less melody or variation throughout the line
7. Don't over-sell

To understand these principles, in the following examples, let your voice follow the arrows at the end of each sentence. First is the traditional "announcer" read. Notice how the lines end *up* or straight.

The seating on this plane is the most comfortable seating on a plane today. ↑

The cost to fly on this airline is the most economical in the industry. →

Join us and sit in the lap of air travel luxury. ↑

With more savings. →

More space. ↑

Free movies. ↑

And more friendly service. →

The choice is simple, pay less and fly with the best. ↑

Now, take the announcer read out. Notice how the lines end *down* or straight.

The seating on this plane is the most comfortable seating on a plane today. ↓

The cost to fly on this airline is the most economical in the industry. →

Join us and sit in the lap of air travel luxury. ↓

With more savings. →

More space. →

Free movies. →

And more friendly service. ↓

The choice is simple, pay less and fly with the best. ↓

Another way to take the announcer read out of promo copy is to change rhythm. Sometimes, the traditional announcer rhythm is fast, choppy, and succinct with a marching tempo. When you change the rhythm to a flowing, trot-like, gliding tempo, you bring a natural pace to the read that makes it more soothing and less frantic.

If I were to use playing the drums as an analogy, I would say to use brushes instead of drumsticks. Think smooth jazz instead of up-tempo rock-and-roll.

Please, don't totally abandon your ability to read announcer copy like a traditional announcer. A trend is just a trend and they are forever changing.

CHAPTER **12**

Roadblocks

When you sit down to record a piece of copy for an audition or at an actual job, after having warmed up with some of my tongue twisters, peruse the copy and look for " verbal land mines"—tough words and passages that may pose a tongue-twisting challenge to you.

Example: An accent is easy to accept as long as it is **accessed accurately ascending in ascension to esthetics ethics and essential essence irrevocable irreconcilable indescribably indelibly delectable and irascibly** contrived to the point of incredulous simultaneous combustion at the risk of salutations that rise above the lifeless lineless numbness of the vernacular.

The boldfaced text is a mouthful and could pose a problem in a session if you haven't practiced. But if you have practiced the passage over and over again before the session, the potential buried explosive device will not trap you. The "land mine" will be a fizzled-out dud and the words will roll off of your lips with a smooth confidence that can only be achieved when you look for the roadblocks in the script.

"If you're trying to achieve, there will be roadblocks. I've had them; everybody has had them. But obstacles don't have to stop you. If you run into a wall, don't turn around and give up. Figure out how to climb it, go through it, or work around it."
—Michael Jordan

CHAPTER **13**

Video-Game Voiceover

VIDEO GAMES ARE ONE OF THE HOTTEST GENRES IN VOICE-over; so it would behoove you to develop the skills to participate in this area of the business. You will need to take some improvisation classes, acting classes, and voiceover classes.

Also, work on developing a wide range of voices. If there are any accents or impersonations that you excel at, they will come in handy for video games. Every character has a rhythm. If a character is dark, you tend to speak in a minor key; and a bright, major key when the role calls for a brighter, happier voice.

Casting directors are impressed with talented actors who have the ability to voice multiple roles. Develop an old voice, a young voice, different nationalities, animals, robots, kids, etc. It's a known fact in Hollywood that the more versatile you are the more casting directors will want to hire you.

> "There is so much to do within a video game that you need to schedule the session for the end of the week. There are so many lines that you need the weekend to recover."
> —John DiMaggio, in the documentary *I Know That Voice*

WHAT HAPPENS IN A VIDEO-GAME SESSION

Video game sessions can last anywhere from one hour to four hours. You could work on a game that calls you back for several more sessions to complete what is needed from your character to finish the game.

Be prepared to do "pick-ups" (re-do a line or extra lines). You should also have an understanding of how to pull off sounds of battle, taking punches, bullets, feeling pain, etc. There is a difference between the effort sounds you make to take a punch from the sound you make to deliver a punch. A good video game voice actor will learn the techniques needed to accomplish these sounds and efforts.

The engineer will conduct a microphone check for each actor. He will instruct you to shout as loud as you might shout during the game and he will also ask you to read some of your dialog as he makes level adjustments to your individual microphone.

Sometimes, the director will have a read-through rehearsal before recording the session, but generally the session begins as scheduled.

Video game acting can be physical and requires at least an average level of physical fitness—especially when video game producers use Motion Capture Technology. As Jennifer Hale says in the documentary *I Know That Voice*, "The visuals [in games] are getting better and better, especially as we get more mo-cap."

When motion capture technology is used, the actor is dressed in a leotard with integral reflective or magnetic markers attached to it. The actor performs the actions that are required and the digital cameras—or an array of cameras—capture the motion of the reflective markers. The end product gives the effect of animated characters acting directly with human actors. Sometimes this requires vigorous movement. You have to be in shape.

"The obvious objective of video games is to entertain people by surprising them with new experiences."
—Shigeru Miyamato

VIDEO-GAME TONGUE TWISTERS

Use this tongue twister to warm up for video game copy.

See how quickly you can say these sentences aloud without tripping up.

> Victors violently viciously venomously vehemently vigorously vie for victory.

Faster now ...

> Victors violently viciously venomously vehemently vigorously vie for victory.

And even faster ...
   Victors violently viciously venomously vehemently vigorously vie for victory.

Great! Now try this one.
   Jungle rumble tumble fumble stumble
   Jungle rumble tumble fumble stumble
   Jungle rumble tumble fumble stumble

Here's another ...
   He tried to trick the twister with his own tongue twister but ended up tie-tongued tripped up triple twined and totally twisted.

And one more ....
   Bombastically bury them on the beaches
   Strategically strike the enemy down
   Bombard and obliterate in the air
   Smash and smolder on the ground

Now, let's practice the dialogue you might find in a typical script for a video game session. Most of these lines are mainly shouted or projected.

"Let me know when it is time for war!"

"Smoke them out ... Hunt them down ... Leave no rock unturned!"

[*said while grinning*] "Ain't nothing but a party!"

[*said with wide eyes*] "Oh, man!"

[*said with rising anger*] "I will blast you into oblivion!"

[*said while pulling out a gun*] "And you will join me there … move out now!"

[*said with quiet anger*] "You sorry, pathetic fool."

[*said with undying loyalty*] "I will follow your command, sir."

[*said while holding a gun*] "Let the combat begin!"

[*said while pulling out a gun*] "Who wants to be the first to die?"

"Medic, medic, I've been hit!"

"Your move, sucker."

"Is that all you got?"

"Incoming! Incoming!"

"Secure the perimeter!"

"The enemy is approaching—fall in line!"

Practice different tongue twisters using different voices. Your ability to do different voices will really come in handy in video games and animation where you are expected to be able to do several different characters in a given session.

PHYSICALITY IN VIDEO-GAME WORK

It is important to be physical when you work on video games, so when you warm-up with your tongue twisters, be sure to move in front of the microphone. Notice the VO direction in brackets. When I worked on *SOCOM 4 U.S. Navy Seals*, the director Kris Zimmerman made sure I put real physicality into every line that I spoke. For instance, if the script called for me to hold a rifle, she would insist that I hold my arms and hands in a rifle-holding position.

"Acting is the physical representation of a mental picture and the projection of an emotional concept."
—Laurette Taylor

PLAY VIDEO GAMES: EARN A COLLEGE SCHOLARSHIP!

In case you needed one more reason to practice video game tongue twisters and vocal warm-ups, you should know that there are now college scholarships awarded for video game play! That's right! Students can earn a scholarship based on their ability to play video games.

Why? Because a game like *League of Legends* (fans of the game call it *LoL*) has 70 million players per month and it was the most popular video game in the U.S. and Europe in 2012. Since *LoL* is designed for large-scale competition, players from around the world combine into teams to battle on the virtual battlefield. These players spent over $624 million in 2014 on in-game purchases.

The University of Pikeville, a private liberal arts college in Kentucky, was the first to make video games an official sport and start offering scholarships to gamers. Robert Morris University in Chicago is the second college that has made the video game an official sport and will offer twenty scholarships to talented students with a certain GPA.

Can you believe it? These students practice and study other gaming teams just like college football teams do!

Now, proceed to the next section on vocal warm-ups so you can better your chances to be cast in a video game that could be the next League of Legends and make you a lot of money!

Here we go!

Section 3

Vocal Warm-Ups

"Before I go on stage, I drink olive oil. It's disgusting, but it's good for your throat. Then I grab my band and we do vocal warm-ups and dance. After that, we put our hands together and say a little prayer."
–SELENA GOMEZ

> "The face is a picture of the mind with eyes as its interpreter."
> —Marcus Tullius Cicero

CHAPTER **14**

Exercising Facial Muscles

IT TAKES GOOD FLEXIBILITY AND DEXTERITY TO SUCCESSFULLY read complicated tongue twisters and other copy. Vocal warm-ups are one of the two most important aspects of your pre-read preparation, and a prerequisite to this is exercising your facial muscles.

Note: **I use the word *warm-up* in reference to vocal exercises and also to introduce reading copy techniques for fast tags, commercials, promos, and trailer copy. If you have the opportunity to get a script before the session, warm up by constantly practicing it using the techniques provided in this book. The bottom line is, the more warmed up you are, the better you are going to be.**

Facial exercises benefit your voice just like regular exercise benefits your body. Try the following facial exercises:

1. Raise your eyebrows as high as you can and hold for five seconds.

2. Open your mouth as wide as possible and stick your tongue out as far as you can; hold for several seconds.

3. Using your three center fingers, press down on your cheeks and smile as hard as you can to raise your cheek muscles against your fingers.

4. Move your nose as much as you can from side to side.

5. Lift your eyebrows as high as you can, open your eyes as wide as possible, and frown at the same time.

6. Pucker your lips out as far as possible into the shape of an O. Then change your expression into a wide smile. Repeat several times.

7. Sit in a comfortable chair and look up at the ceiling. Pucker your lips and stick your tongue out as far as possible to exercise your neck muscles.

CHAPTER **15**

Getting the Most from Vocal Warm-Ups

WARMING UP IS ONE OF THE MOST IMPORTANT THINGS you can do to extend your voiceover career. It is an absolute must to maintain a long, prosperous, and healthy career. As a person who makes a living using your voice, you are no different from a boxer, baseball or basketball player—you must warm up the muscles you use to keep them in great working condition. If you are a singer, warm up with musical scales. If you are a stage actor, warm up with lip trills and tongue trills. If you are a voiceover actor, do all of the above and add some of my tongue twisters.

"If you spend too much time warming up, you'll miss the race. If you don't warm up at all, you may not finish the race."
—Grand Heidrich

Here are some other things to consider when you begin your day by warming up properly.

GOOD POSTURE

Posture is very important when it comes to warming up your voice. I came up in the theater where I had to project to the last person in the back of the house in the mezzanine and the balcony. My voice had to be placed properly in the vocal mask and I had to breathe properly using my diaphragm to support every word that came out of my mouth.

None of this could have been accomplished without good posture, whether I was standing or sitting erect. When you sing musical scales or just open your mouth and say ahhhh you will have better results if you have good posture.

Bad posture restricts the flow of your breathing and vocal delivery. Good posture lets everything flow freely.

ROOM-TEMPERATURE WATER

There is nothing like a cool glass of liquid on a hot summer day or after a vigorous physical workout. Your body heats up in both instances and craves a cool dose of relief. On the other hand, vocal cords never ever crave such a remedy when they are in need of a refresher.

The voice craves warmth, moisture, and something soothing. Room-temperature water is perfect. It's not harsh and it doesn't influence pitch or vocal clarity. It just soothes the vocal cords. Warm teas are also good.

THE POWER OF THE HUM

As a singer, I was always taught to make sure my voice was placed in the mask. I was told to sing in a way that I would feel resonance in the mask with my voice coming out of my mouth without strain or improper use of my throat muscles.

Well, the ideal way to find out what it feels like when you are properly speaking or singing from the mask is to hum.

Take the resonance and sensation that you feel from the hum and work on getting that same resonance with every word that comes out of your mouth, and you will be projecting from the right place.

Here are some comments from one of my students, Thomas Dunn, who shares with us his warm-up regimen which includes tongue twisters.

Thomas Dunn, Voice Actor

Vocal warm-ups are very important to me before recording an audition or studio session. I practice several different techniques, but one of the most effective for me is the tongue twister.

I start by reading the tongue twister silently to familiarize myself with the words and cadence. Then I read the tongue twister aloud slowly several times, as many times as I need, to say each word and phrase correctly.

As I read, I begin to visualize the words and phrases, because the clearer the image is in my mind, the easier it is to read. If I can see it, I can say it.

Once I have a good picture in mind and I am able to read the tongue twister perfectly, I slowly start to increase the speed of the read. If I stumble, then I reduce the speed until I can read it perfectly every time.

If I tire of reading the same twister, I move on to another one using the same technique. Once I have at least a whole page of twisters, I start from the top and read them at whatever pace allows me to do them all perfectly.

I find that memorizing the tongue twister helps me repeat them easier and faster as I practice. I take a break every so often to allow my brain to absorb and catalog the phrases.

The more I repeat the tongue twisters, the more I train my tongue, lips, and cheeks to navigate through even the trickiest ad copy.

Oh, I always have a bottle of room-temperature water handy and sip it often.

"A sharp tongue is the only edge tool that grows keener with constant use."
—Washington Irving

Repeat this cadence of words. Start off slowly and make sure your face, jaws, lips, and tongue are relaxed. Gradually increase your speed.

    Heidi He
    Heidi Ho
    Papalee Papalo

ALWAYS WARM UP YOUR VOICE BEFORE SPEAKING

All vocal warm-ups don't fit every voiceover artist which is why I include different tongue twisters and warm-ups in this book for different types of voiceover work. Are you getting ready to read promo copy? Go to one of the promo warm-ups. Want to warm up for a trailer read? Go to one of the trailer tongue twisters or vocal warm-ups.

All of the exercises in this book are designed to help you overcome and correct a problem and enhance the good things you already do with your wonderful voice.

I know you are anxious to get on with the show—but by all means, I insist that you warm up before you speak!

Here is a morning vocal workout you can use to take your mouth through every motion it will go through while reading copy throughout the day, from open-vowel sounds, to the resonance from a hum, to flapping lips, and using your tongue as it strikes the roof of your mouth. Every motion that you will incur in a session is exercised and warmed up with this workout. Give it a try.

Let's start with some open-vowel warm ups.
  A . . . E . . . Ah . . . O . . . Ohh
  A . . . E . . . Ah . . . O . . . Ohh
  A . . . E . . . Ah . . . O . . . Ohh
  A . . . E . . . Ah . . . O . . . Ohh

Now open and close your mouth with this ho-hum exercise. Be sure to close your mouth and over enunciate the word "Hum."
  Hee . . . Hi . . . Hum Ho Hum
  Hee . . . Hi . . . Hum Ho Hum
  Hee . . . Hi . . . Hum Ho Hum

Now flip and flop your lips with these words.
    Flip flop flip flap flip
    Flip flop flip flap flop
    Flip flop flip flap flop

Let your tongue get used to touching the roof of your mouth with these words.
    Tip Top Tiny Tot Tutu Tout
    Tip Top Tiny Tot Tutu Tout
    Tip Top Tiny Tot Tutu Tout

Repeat this sequence for ten to fifteen minutes and you will be ready to speak. Finally, end this warm-up with the tough tongue twister below. Read it at a good pace but clarity is most important.

The third time the two-tongued turquoise turtle told the teeny tiny tortuous that together they took three times ten times three times one time to tip toe thirty three times together tentatively through the tulips.

    Great job!

"If you warm up properly you're not going to get hurt and if you warm down properly you're not going to get hurt."
—Charlie Adler

THE APPROACH

Whenever you prepare to warm up your voice by reading a tongue twister, you need to approach the exercise with a couple of intentions in mind. First, you need to know what you are trying to accomplish. Are you looking for a vocal warm-up? Are you practicing a certain group of words that start with *th* or *pl*? Perhaps you just want to loosen your jaw muscles. Make up your mind and have a purpose. Once you know what your intent is, approach the appropriate tongue twisters.

With that in mind, you should become familiar with these common vocal warm-up mistakes so you can avoid them:

1. Not taking time to comprehend the material
2. Not articulating
3. Over-working your vocal cords
4. Using the wrong vocal exercises

Every voiceover professional finds the warm-up method that works best for him or her. For instance, to warm up vocally, animation actor and director Charlie Adler sings on his way to work before a session, and he repeats the process after the session.

THE NEED FOR ENERGY

A critical aspect of reading voiceover copy is your energy level. Sometimes the amount of energy needed verbally is displayed in the VO direction. Sometimes it is indicated in the written words; but regardless of the source, energy is always present when you read copy.

A great source of energy level can come from your tongue-twister workout. You can work various speeds that will get your adrenalin up and, in turn, increase your energy level before you read copy.

AVOID STRAINING YOUR MUSCLES

I can't stress enough how important it is to warm up before you do voiceover work. Although I think it is best to do something immediately before you start a session, you can also warm up first thing in the morning, around lunchtime, and even after dinner.

The point is, you must warm up your vocal muscles to prepare them for the strenuous day that includes every conversation you have, every song you sing, and every piece of copy you read. There is a lot of vocal tension involved in all of these activities. You need to avoid damaging you sensitive vocal cords by making sure you are always properly warmed up.

Speaking of technique, let's explore the art of the conversational read ...

CHAPTER **16**

The Ramp-Up ... and the Groove

One of the new trends in voiceover is the conversational or "real person" read. Well, it has been around for a long time for commercials, but now producers are starting to request this style for promo and narration reads as well.

> "Speak clearly, if you speak at all;
> carve every word before you let it fall."
> —Oliver Wendell Holmes

It is really important to learn a few techniques to get you in the right place and frame of mind to execute this request. One great technique is called the "Ramp-Up." Using the copy below, here is how it works:

The VO direction for the narration copy is: *Please read with a conversational friendly tone. No announcers please.* In order to understand what you're being asked to avoid, first read this narration like an announcer (even though that is exactly what the director does not want.)

Please read with a conversational friendly tone. No announcers please.

Mindful

I am mindful of my creator
My good Lord and savior
For all he has provided
And brought me through

I am mindful of my blessings
My home and my dressings
My ability to function
As well as I do

What more can I ask for?
Don't know that I need more
So satisfied with all he has done

His love is so perfect
Don't know that I am worth it
But I will keep on doing
All that he wants me to do

Now read it again but add the introductory sentence in your own conversational voice before you get into the copy. "Let me tell you something really great about how I feel..."

Let me tell you something really great about how I feel ...

Mindful

I am mindful of my creator
My good Lord and savior
For all he has provided
And brought me through

I am mindful of my blessings
My home and my dressings
My ability to function
As well as I do

What more can I ask for?
Don't know that I need more
So satisfied with all he has done

His love is so perfect
Don't know that I am worth it
But I will keep on doing
All that he wants me to do

Now add the name of a relative or a friend to the end of the same sentence—"Let me tell you something really great about how I feel, John" or "Let me tell you something really great about how I feel, Aunt Karen" and go from there right into the copy.

Let me tell you something great about how I feel, _____

Mindful

I am mindful of my creator
My good Lord and savior
For all he has provided
And brought me through

I am mindful of my blessings
My home and my dressings
My ability to function
As well as I do

What more can I ask for?
Don't know that I need more
So satisfied with all he has done

His love is so perfect
Don't know that I am worth it
But I will keep on doing
All that he wants me to do

Did you notice how using the upfront ad lib and/or adding someone's name put you in a more natural, conversational place? Were you able to continue that tone throughout the read?

That is one example of how to Ramp Up into the copy and achieve a non-announcer conversational "real-person" read. You can also use the Ramp-Up method before you do a tongue twister and thus make your vocal warm-up closer to what you will be doing during the audition or session.

Read the tongue twister copy below once in your announcer voice.

> The birds and the bumble bees
> The flowers and the sycamore trees
> The crescent moon up above
> And a thing called love

Add the following line and read it in a more conversational tone: "Did I ever tell you that I really get a kick out of nature and love? Seriously, I really do." Then go from there into the copy.

> Did I ever tell you that I really get a kick out of nature and love?
> Seriously, I really do ....
> The birds and the bumble bees
> The flowers and the sycamore trees
> The crescent moon up above
> And a thing called love

... AND THE GROOVE

I started out singing when I was just a little kid in Detroit. My parents tell me I was singing complete Motown songs at the early age of two.

I went on to act in high school musicals. I had the lead role in three fabulous musicals during my years at Henry Ford High. I was Tony in *Westside Story*, Sky Masterson in *Guys and Dolls*, and Billy Bigelow in *Carousel*. For as long as I can remember, everything for me has been set in a tempo, a groove. There was a rhythm to the music, there was rhythm in the words.

When I performed on Broadway and later in Hollywood on television, I was always engulfed in the tempo, the rhythm, and the groove. That same groove exists in voiceover copy and once you set the groove, you have to stay in it. The tempo might change, the cadence might change—but you must never ever lose the groove.

The groove is your interpretation. Once your interpretation is set, you have to commit to it, believe in it, and never abandon it during your read.

"I've always associated what I do to singing without music."
—Don LaFontaine

CHAPTER **17**

Personalization

B ASKETBALL PLAYERS HAVE A GO-TO MOVE. THEY HAVE a shot they take and a certain way they move to take the shot every time they shoot it. Why? Because they are successful with this go-to move more often than not.

Likewise, Frank Sinatra's signature song was "My Way." He usually closed his shows with that song and it always got a big round of applause. Where would Santa Claus be without his hearty Ho, Ho, Ho? Or Superman without his cape?

The point is, you need to find a tongue twister and vocal warm-up that is perfect for you. Find a favorite routine and commit it to memory.

"You must make every piece of copy your own. When you make it personal, you own it."
—Rodney Saulsberry

Before I started creating my own tongue twisters, my "personalization tongue twisters" were *Lips teeth tip of the tongue* and *Red letter yellow leather*. I still use those, but I also added others of my own creation to my collection.

With the practice of personalization, you will never be without a vocal warm-up or tongue twister on the tip of your tongue, because your favorites will be committed to memory.

OBJECTIVES AND EXPECTATIONS

Before we go any further, let's talk briefly about our objectives and expectations from practicing tongue twisters. The objective is to become adept at picking up any piece of copy, hard or easy, and reading it with the flair, panache, and vocal dexterity of the most gifted of tongue; to bring color and variety to long-form narration and to read scientific and medical prose with the ease of a children's bedtime story. The constant speaking of these verbal gymnastic rhymes and riddles creates an ability to not only read better, but to even write your own tongue twisters that meet your immediate needs or that you simply want to share with others and have fun with.

Whatever your objectives or expectations, you have to work really hard to accomplish your goal.

"I never paint what is,
I only paint what I imagine could be."
—Degas

Section 4

Mic Technique & Other Tips

> "Technique is noticed most markedly in the case of those who have not mastered it."
> –LEON TROTSKY

"All our dreams can come true—
if we have the courage to pursue them."
—Walt Disney

CHAPTER **18**

Getting the Most from the Mic

THE MICROPHONE IS ONE OF THE MOST CRITICAL PARTS of the recording process. A top-quality microphone will provide you with the basis for excellent audio. A microphone amplifies your voice, but you also have to know how to finesse it and remember that it is not a substitute for good vocal expression. You still need to interpret the copy and be exciting if that is what the copy calls for. You must also learn the techniques of good microphone use.

HOW TO TALK INTO A MICROPHONE

First of all, you should decide if you want to sit or stand comfortably. If you are too close to the microphone, it will distort, so find the proper distance.

If you watch singers perform, you will notice how they tend

to pull their hand-held microphones back when they start to sing louder. That is because they don't want to overload and distort the microphone.

SIT OR STAND?

When I first started doing voiceovers, I always stood because that is the way I addressed the microphone as a singer and I believed that everything a singer does in relation to the microphone is what a voiceover actor should also do. Plus, it made sense when you think about proper breathing and the ability to let your erect posture assist you in getting out every ounce of your voice when you speak.

However, when I got older, I started sitting more. I would say I probably sit sixty percent of the time these days with good erect posture and I don't notice any difference in my voice performance, stamina, or overall output.

At the end of the day, sitting or standing is a personal choice.

USB MICROPHONES

A USB microphone connects directly to a computer or laptop through an available USB port on the computer. Combined with recording software like Pro Tools, Audacity, or Twisted Wave, the user records the audio that the microphone picks up and can then edit and save the audio on the computer.

There are a few advantages to the USB microphone and some disadvantages over traditional microphones. The first key benefit is that a USB microphone does not require a separate adapter or mixing board because it plugs directly into the computer. The microphone is powered by the USB connection and audio data is transferred directly through the USB connection.

However, there are some people who believe the USB connection does not provide studio-quality audio recording. A high-end studio microphone and a studio mixer are needed to get studio-quality recordings according to a *Macworld* review of USB microphones.

I agree. A USB mic is not the same quality as a high-end studio microphone but it's good and it will suffice in the interim before you purchase an expensive, high-end studio microphone.

RECOMMENDED MICROPHONES

The Yeti is one of the most advanced and versatile multi-pattern USB microphones available anywhere. Combining three capsules and four different pattern settings, the Yeti is an ultimate tool for creating amazing recordings directly to your computer. With exceptional sound and performance, the Yeti can capture anything with a clarity and ease unheard of in a USB microphone.

A microphone for the iPad, iPhone, and Mac is a mic manufactured by Apogee. About the size of an iPhone, this microphone makes it easy to capture your best take with incredible quality.

The microphone that is installed in iPhones, from the iPhone 4 to whatever is the latest version on the market, is exceptional and will do in a pinch if you can't get to a so-called high quality mic in a studio. I have recorded several auditions in my car on my iPhone and the results have been phenomenal. (Several auditions on that microphone have led to jobs.) The camera and the video camera are also excellent on the iPhone.

Personally, I use the Sennheiser MKH 416, a shotgun interference tube microphone. Its excellent directional ability and compact design, high-consonant articulation, and feedback rejection make the MKH one of the best. I also use USB microphones that include a Snowball by Blue Microphones and the Apogee.

CARING FOR YOUR MICROPHONES

Obey the normal common-sense rules of electronic equipment care (e.g., avoid very high temperatures, dust, dampness, high humidity, physical shocks, etc). Additionally:

- Don't blow into the mic, because the diaphragm is designed to respond to sound waves, not wind.
- Don't tap the head of the microphone, because this can damage the mic.
- Don't subject microphones to volume levels greater than their design capabilities.

CHAPTER **19**

Vocal Care

D O YOU KNOW HOW IMPORTANT YOUR VOICE IS? IN MOST professions, it is your first form of communication; and it certainly is in voiceover, acting, singing, and public speaking. Many people judge you by the sound of your voice. You need to be concerned about how you sound and what your voice might convey about your ability to deliver what a commercial, promo or video game requires.

With so much responsibility and expectations thrust on your voice, the proper care of it is paramount. Respect your instrument, because your voice is the key to your success.

"If I get a cold I can still work. I get some Sinex or something to clear my throat and I work."
—Don LaFontaine

PHYSICAL FITNESS, DIET, AND SLEEP

Physical fitness keeps your voice healthy. When I got healthier, it improved my stamina. I became stronger in my strenuous video-game sessions and my energy while reading long narration improved greatly.

Physical exercise raises endorphins and makes one feel happier and healthier. It is certainly an easy and effective way to boost your self-confidence.

Here's a specific diet tip for voiceover artists—don't drink milk or eat yogurt before a session. Dairy products will clog your throat. I try not to ever drink or eat dairy products before I work.

Rest is also very important. If you're tired during a session, you can hear it. My auditions and sessions are much better when I get at least six hours of sleep at night. If for some reason I don't get six hours, a twenty- to thirty-minute power nap in the afternoon gives me the boost I need to be at my best for the remainder of the day. During a power nap, you don't have to be in a deep sleep, just resting will do the trick.

BREATHE LIKE A SINGER

As I discussed in chapter 3, you need to learn how to support your voice by breathing correctly and using your diaphragm. Most breathing and vocal techniques used by singers also work for voiceover artists. And don't forget that when you sing, your stomach should expand as you inhale and contract as you exhale. The same thing should happen when you speak. The breathing principles and techniques are identical.

VOCALIZE

You should warm up every day, especially before an audition or a session. I do. Here is the URL for one of my popular vocal warm-up videos on YouTube: Youtube.com/watch?v=GoRyRbyKKOU

VOCAL REST

One of the best remedies for whatever ails you is rest. When you completely stop using your voice for several hours at a time, you increase the possibility of getting your full voice back more quickly.

"If you neglect to recharge a battery, it dies. And if you run full speed ahead without stopping for water, you lose momentum to finish the race."
—Oprah Winfrey

HYDRATION

Do you know how important hydration is? There have been times in my life when I wasn't feeling well and when I saw our family doctor, I was told I was suffering from dehydration. The simple remedy for this problem: drink water.

Hydration is critical when it comes to taking care of your voice. If you want to stay hydrated, you need to drink water.

How much? According to the Institute of Medicine (by way of the Mayo Clinic), men need roughly three quarts per day (thirteen 8-ounce cups), while women need about 2.2 quarts (9 cups) of fluid.

Some people believe that too much water is not good either. My personal experience has been to try to drink at least a quart of water a day and whenever I am thirsty. I feel better when I drink water and it's good for my vocal chords.

Your vocal chords need to be lubricated with a thin layer of mucus in order to vibrate efficiently—and the best lubrication is achieved by drinking plenty of water. By all means, stay hydrated.

LIQUIDS TO AVOID

Some fluids can cause or exacerbate dehydration, including caffeinated drinks like coffee and soft drinks. Alcohol completely dries me out, especially vodka.

Be wise and don't consume any of these drinks before a session.

CHAPTER **20**

Allergies and Sinus Care

WHEN I DECIDED TO WRITE THIS BOOK, IT WAS important to me to include contributions from my students and other people who had read my first two books.

With that in mind, I asked voiceover actors to share with me what they did to maintain vocal care as they operated in the business every day, both auditioning and working. Following are some of their tips which I am sure will be helpful to you.

"A guitarist or a drummer can get a cold and still play; I get a cold and sound like a wet mitten trying to sing a love song. Charming."

–Tori Amos

Disclaimer: *I am not a member of the medical profession, and neither are any of the voiceover professionals who generously contributed to this section. Any advice about healthcare offered in this book should be considered purely anecdotal. In other words, we are simply sharing with you what works for us. Please consult a physician before using any medication and before making any changes to your diet or physical routine.*

Fred North, Voice Actor

"I use a nasal relief sinus wash each morning to clear my sinuses and to limit post nasal drip. It is a nasal rinse squeeze bottle with nasal rinse salt packets and DISTILLED water. Do not use tap water, it can be a health issue.

"Recently I began adding a product called Alkalol nasal wash to the saline rinse. The squeeze bottle and salt packets can be purchased at most any pharmacy. (I've only found the Alkalol at CVS.) I find the combo very effective.

"I also use it after outdoor activity like running, mowing, golf, etc. to clear the allergens from my sinuses. The whole process is a little weird at first but the result more than compensates for the short-term oddity of blasting the product up your nostrils. Just breathe through your mouth while doing it and it will go up one nostril and out the other.

"I also take an over-the-counter antihistamine every day, but I avoid decongestants because they can dry out my throat and cause me other issues as well.

"The above process is the first thing that has truly and consistently helped me."

Ron Devon, Voiceover Actor and Singer

"For the record, I have been performing professionally for thirty-six years and have appeared from Detroit to Chicago to Las Vegas. I have a 3 to 3.5 octave range and perform live on average of just over twenty hours a week. In 2013, I did well over 200 shows and my performances average five hours a night. I have not lost a day to vocal issues for at least two years.

"I have carefully designed my first set to gradually warm up my voice. Nothing hard or strenuous in the first hour. I practice "speech level singing," originally developed by Seth Riggs. The idea is you should never sing any harder than you speak. Singing is "talking on pitch." His methods can be valuable to people who talk for a living.

"Obviously, don't smoke and don't drink! I don't smoke at all and only have very small quantities of alcohol, if any, AFTER a show or on a day I don't have to perform.

"Drink only room-temperature water and don't eat a big meal within a few hours of performance.

"I use food-grade glycerin in my water bottle. Glycerin is used by the body to draw moisture into muscle tissue. The vocal chords are muscles. The glycerin helps keep them well lubricated. It can be found at most health food stores. Remember it takes twenty minutes for whatever you drink to get to your throat … so start drinking water well before you have to perform.

"If I am having any struggles, I will use Honey Loquat Syrup, available online or at better health food stores. This sweet, very thick, syrup gives a tremendous coating to the throat and is medicinal for what ails you.

"For colds, I use an old mountain recipe: whisky, honey and lemon. Mix in equal parts and use to fight the cold.

"If you are losing your voice, DON'T WHISPER!! Whispering puts extra strain on your voice and exacerbates the situation.

"Find a good otolaryngologist (ear, nose throat doctor) who understands what you do for a living. Preferably one who specializes in the throat and voice.

"Buy a good steam inhaler. Steam is remarkable for its ability to cut through congestion and fight inflammation in the throat. I use the Vicks Personal Steam Inhaler and I've heard good things about the MyPurMist inhaler. I know, for example, Sting, uses an inhaler every night before he goes onstage just to make sure his throat is warm and moist.

"If you have a humidifier on your house heating system, set it to 35 to40 percent during the dry winter months. (This is for those of us living in the upper Midwest!)

"If you're going to your kid's ballgame—no matter how well he/she does—DO NOT SHOUT! Use your hands to show your approval!"

Christi Bowen, Voice Actor

"Vocal health is a really important part of the job to me. I've had some issues in the past and I know how important taking care of my instrument can be. I drink lots of water, don't scream, avoid dairy ... all the usual things.

"Warming up is the first thing I do every morning. I wouldn't record without it. I do scales, lip trills, neck and face stretches, and of course tongue twisters—many of which are Rodney originals!"

Joe Loesch, Voice Actor

"First, I try not to get colds by taking care of myself, eating right, and taking vitamins. But there are times when you're around others who are sick. Sometimes you just can't avoid it. Especially when someone tells you they have a sinus condition and you know darned well they have a cold!

"When this happens and the cold hits, I'll have a cup of hot water with three teaspoons of Apple Cider Vinegar (the real stuff, not processed) and a teaspoon of pure honey. Two of these doses back to back, three times daily and you'll find that you've cut your cold's visit to half the time of its usual stay."

Mike Elmore, Voice Actor

"I've been in the radio/voiceover arena for decades now. As long as I can remember people have asked me what I do to take care of my voice. Or more specifically what THEY can do to take care of their voice. My answer is always: 'For me, it's not so much what I DO as much as it is what I DON'T DO.' I have never been a smoker or a heavy drinker. Those are things I have been told by many will certainly alter your vocal folds thus your sound. People that start doing voiceovers as a smoker find that if and when they decide to make a move towards overall better health and quit, they have to pretty much learn some areas of vocal control all over again. They are playing a new instrument."

TIPS FROM THE DOCUMENTARY
I KNOW THAT VOICE

David Kaye

"I use Alcolol, not alcohol, Alcolol. It's a throat rinse that has been around since the late 1800s."

Bob Bergen

"I use a thing called Entertainers Secret. It's an herbal spray."

Debi Derryberry

"Have your session when your voice is not tired. You can't go to a football game and scream and expect to get in front of a microphone the next day."

Debi Derryberry

"It is an instrument; so you have to keep it warmed up."

Section 5

More Tongue Twisters

"Excellence is more than just a skill, it is an attitude."
–RODNEY SAULSBERRY

"All parts of the human body get tired eventually—
except the tongue."
—Konrad Adenauer

CHAPTER **21**

Twisters for Specific Genres

Now THAT YOU HAVE HONED YOUR BASIC TONGUE-twisting skills, did vocal warm-ups, and learned about vocal care, it's time to get back to having fun with more tricky text!

The purpose of the tongue twisters, poems, and vocal exercises in this book is to give you the opportunity to warm up before a particular read or to just practice saying the words that generally come up in the particular genre that you are reading. In this chapter, I provide poems and other tongue twisters that are specific to promo, trailer, and other voice-over genres.

And so, if you are reading a commercial, practice with a commercial tongue twister. If you are preparing to read a promo, warm up with a promo tongue twister that embodies the general words that you may be asked to read. It just so happens that not only is this a beneficial exercise, you get to have a lot of fun in the process.

And, as I said earlier, all of the tongue twisters, poems, and vocal exercises in this book were created by me except where noted.

Enjoy the challenges ahead!

MOVIE-TRAILER TONGUE TWISTERS

Let's start with a poem that sets the mood for movie-trailer exercises.

Cinematic Poetry

Cinema tracker movie spectacular
Sequel equal blockbuster vehicle
Money-maker box office breaker
And how to read a trailer

Mover shaker comedy caper
Drama trauma Bahama mama
A good review from me to you
And how to read a trailer

Tear-jerker counter worker
Popping corn without the butter
Horror scenes with screaming teens
And how to read a trailer
Matt Damon, Tom Cruise

Will Smith is breaking news
Sticky gum on the bottom of your shoes
Funky music and the blues
Foreign films are hard to sell
Bigger names will never fail
Morgan Freeman and Denzel
And how to read a trailer

READ THE COPY BACKWARD

In this exercise we read common trailer lines as we know them and then we read the same line backwards. This may seem awkward and useless but it really helps you practice and retain common trailer-copy jargon that is used quite often in a trailer voiceover session.

Now playing in theaters everywhere

Everywhere theaters in playing now

Starts Friday at a theater near you

You near theater a at Friday starts

Starts tomorrow

Tomorrow starts

Rated PG13

13PG rated

Some material may be inappropriate for children under 13

13 under children for inappropriate be may material some

Here's a tongue twister to get you warmed up to say female movie star names in a trailer.

Read with pace.

Betty B

Betty b biaz Cameron Diaz
Betty b beep Meryl Streep
Betty b bolie Angelina Jolie
Betty b bison Cicely Tyson
Betty b bobbers Julia Roberts
Betty b binslet Kate Winslet
Betty b bank Hilary Swank
Betty b bippin Nicole Kidman
Betty b bannison Jennifer Aniston
Betty b perry Halle Berry

Here's a tongue twister to get you warmed up to say male movie star names in a trailer.

Read with pace.

Bobby B

Bobby b balken Christopher Walken
Bobby b brockington Denzel Washington
Bobby b britt Brad Pitt
Bobby b blooper Bradley Cooper
Bobby b blind Chris Pine
Bobby b batum Channing Tatum
Bobby b beatman Morgan Freeman
Bobby b bino Al Pacino
Bobby b beeson Liam Neeson
Bobby b beatle Don Cheadle

MORE EXERCISES FOR TRAILER READS

Practice the studio "Presents" phrase

Paramount Pictures presents ...

Universal Pictures presents...

Twentieth Century Fox is proud to present ...

New Line Cinema presents...

Repeat each tag below three times, getting faster each time.

Now playing. Rated R for strong language and images of drugs, violence, and sex. Children under 17 not admitted without parent. Inappropriate for children under 17.

Practice giving each actor equal vocal billing. That means equal emphasis on each name.

Twentieth Century Fox is proud to present ...
Angela Bassett
Taye Diggs
And Whoopi Goldberg

Universal Pictures Presents:
Alfre Woodard
And introducing Zelda Harris

"Crooklyn"
A Spike Lee Joint!

Read each tag with a lot of enthusiasm
    It's America's #1 Comedy
    It's the #1 comedy in America
    It's the #1 comedy in the country

PROMO TONGUE TWISTERS

Promo is one of the most popular genres in the voiceover field today. Everybody wants to do them and there has never been a more opportune time to do so.

> "Without promotion, something terrible happens . . . nothing!"
>
> —P. T. Barnum

New product that needs to be promoted is popping up everywhere, on cable TV and on the Internet. Promo covers so many areas, including books, games, music, video, and network television. Through the years I have had the pleasure of working on all of the major networks and I am currently doing promo work in the International division of Telemundo.

My point is this: you had better be ready to take advantage of this onslaught of work. Hopefully, you will be lucky and get some promo work in the near future. And when you do, you will be more prepared because you practiced with the tongue twisters and vocal warm-ups in this book.

Remember, you make your own luck. Two-time-Oscar-winning actor Denzel Washington once said, "Luck is when preparation meets opportunity."

Let's get started preparing for your luck with the poem/tongue twisters below.

Start out slow and then read with pace.

Reality TV

Promo copy to promote
A TV show shot on remote
Reality the new frontier
Prepare to watch a new premiere
Got to watch this episode
The greatest story ever told
Promo copy to promote
A TV show shot on remote

Good TV

NHL NFL MLB good TV
NBA CBS NBC good TV
CNN BET PBS good TV
CFL BBC TNT good TV

Network Promo Land

ABC NBC BET on TV. CBS TNT BBC on TV. Breaking news blackout blues weather sports and peoples' views. CNN HLN FOX News is at it again. Political elections and poll corrections. Game shows live and taped. Talk show hosts gay and straight. Cancelations bad reviews network local and cable news. Drama sports and comedy, episodic, scientific, and reality. Channel surfing is your cable working? What is your favorite program of choice? Do you have a charming announcer's voice? Because this is only a fraction of what you will need to know. If you ever plan to promote, a primetime television show!

Start out slow and then read with pace.

Tonight Intros and Tags

Tonight …
Tonight …
Tonight …

Tonight on ABC …
Tonight on FOX …
Tonight on CBS …

Tonight at 6/7 Central on Lifetime
Tonight at 8/7 Central on Showtime
Tonight at 9 on HBO

"To me, working out is literally like eating a meal or drinking water or breathing."

—Hillary Swank

This next group of tongue twisters are a lot of fun, and yet really test your skills. I would refer to some of them as being a "Vocal Workout." Give them all a try!

Seven Seals

Seven nauseous seasick seals sailed solo with sixteen seashells and seven soft shell succulent scrumptious shrimp.

The Clipped King

A catatonic chronic clipper clipped cute curly curls completely clasping crooked scissor cutters cleverly around the crescent crown of the cleanly shaven king.

Sonny Sheldon

Sonny Sheldon Sugarman told Sherry Sheperd Pete that if she wanted to remain slender sleek she should not eat sugar sweet shredded wheat off of a shimmering sugar shredded snow white sugar sprinkled solitary cookie sheet.

Red Roses

Rosy red roses require resistance requisites recently resilient resourceful and richly righteous.

Sport Shops

Superior sport shops stock shiny sequined sweat suits and super soft sweat socks.

Flip It

Statistical statistics statistically flip it
Numerical numerals numerically flip it
Political politics politically flip it
Regimental regiments regimentally flip it
Rudimentary rudimental rudiments flip it
Detrimental detriments detrimentally flip it
Propaganda propagate populate flip it

The Big Ship Rudy

Welcome aboard the great big ship where a seaman name Rudy jumped off for a dip. He swam all around the deep blue sea to see all the sights that he could see. What happened to Rudy no one could say cause he never returned on that cold winter day. So in his honor and praise of duty they now call the ship, the big ship Rudy.

Terry Tunnel on Christmas Eve

Terry Tunnel told her teacher Mr. Townsend to teach her how to tie a double knot in the tie of her little brother ten-year-old Timothy Theodore Tunnel so that they could both attend the twentieth anniversary of the Tunnel family tree trimming service to be held at the Trinity Tabernacle Testimonial New Bethel Town Church on Tuesday the tenth day of December fourteen days to the day of Christmas Eve a typically totally terrific night to remember.

A Baker Man

A baker opened a cupcake shop in the center of a town

A thousand cupcakes he did make and passed them all around

How many cupcakes do you think a baker man should bake?

As many cupcakes as it takes to make a town feel great!

Effervescent Magnificent

Effervescent magnificent the coolest words I ever met

Effervescent magnificent they feel so good to say

Effervescent magnificent the coolest words I ever met

Effervescent magnificent they brighten up my day

Sonny Scott

Sonny Scott swiftly scooped six vanilla scoops

He made a mistake and dropped a scoop on his shiny new boots

He tried again to slide a scoop down his hungry throat

But ended up dropping the scoop on his natty new coat

New York

You know your work is in New York
New York is where you work you know
Where you work is in New York
You know your work is in New York

Red Light Green Light Blue

Metro driver city rider
Red light green light blue
Country slicker bourbon drinker
Red light green light blue
Alligator see you later
Found it at a zoo
Escalator elevator
Red light green light blue
City blackout no more lights out
What are we to do?
Cross the street and tap your feet
For red light green light blue

Who?

Who what went where
Why where went what
Who what went where who?

Entrepreneur

Entrepreneur entrepreneurial
Wake up tomorrow and eat all your cereal
Entrepreneur entrepreneurial
Never give up on a dream
Entrepreneur entrepreneurial
Wake up tomorrow and eat all your cereal
Entrepreneur entrepreneurial
Never give up on a dream

The Crazy U's

Utter under unicorn
Usher user unsung
Urchin Ulysses uptown
Unity unit unbound
Understanding untidy unrelenting untrue
Undesirable unfit unimpressive unglue
Unify undertake understated unwind
Unite unseat unilaterally unkind
Utmost upside untie undo
Underneath upper under
Universal under use

Magill Magall Magoo

Ripple the rupple the riggity shuffle magill magall magoo

Ripple the rupple the riggity shuffle bitty bang bitty bop bitty boo

Tootaloo tootie tootie tootaloo tootie tootie

Bitty bang bitty bop bitty boo

Ripple the rupple the riggity shuffle magill magall magoo

Bumble Bees

A bumble bee loved a bumble she who lived up in a hive

He was a two-winged bee three wings had she

So they never saw eye to eye

He tried to flirt but it never worked

Every day he circled her hive

Now the two-winged bee and the three-winged she

Are together and their wings make five

Upfront

Upfront back up turn right now switch
Upfront back up turn right now switch
Upfront back up turn right now switch

Share a Meal

Share a meal and make a deal
Grumpy lumpy dumpy frumpy
Share a meal and make a deal
Grumpsy lumpsy dumpsy frumpsy
Share a meal and make a deal
Grumpty lumpty dumpty frumpty
Share a meal and make a deal
Grumpky lumpky dumpky frumpky
Share a meal and make a deal
Grumpky lumpky dumpky frumpky
Share a meal and make a deal
To share a meal with you

"No one plans to get sick or hurt—
I certainly didn't—but most people will need
medical care at some point in their lives."
—Magic Johnson

MEDICAL TONGUE TWISTERS

Do you have to read some medical copy for your next session or audition? Warm up with these tongue twisters. Say each twister two times in a row.

Bladder bladder gallbladder kidney liver lungs

Glands hands knee mouth shoulder knuckles tongue

Anti inflammatory
Anti-enzymic
Antivaccination too
Anthroplasty
Arterial duct
Antibiotically blue

Dehydration medication patella tendinitis
Metacarpals metatarsals brachial chronic bronchitis

Sacrum scapula sciatica
Sacrum scapula sciatica
Sacrum scapula sciatica

CHAPTER **22**

Twisters and Warm-Ups for Singers

SINGERS HAVE OFTEN ASKED ME IF TONGUE TWISTERS are something that can help them—and my answer is a resounding yes. Any exercise that promotes, encourages, and produces better articulation is beneficial to a singer. And that is exactly what tongue twisters do.

"Being a singer is a natural gift. It means I'm using to the highest degree possible the gift that God gave me to use. I'm happy with that."
—Aretha Franklin

When you consider the fact that we have falsettos, chest voices, and head voices in our singer vocabulary, all of those voices are put to use in the vocal execution of tongue twisters.

They also assist with the development of tongue muscle memory for particular vowel sounds.

Do you think it is important for an audience to be able to understand the lyrics that are being sung? Your answer should be yes if you care about the consumer. And this can only be accomplished with good diction and good articulation.

Warming up your singing voice with challenging tongue twisters is important before musical theatre, opera, and other strenuous vocal performances. Not only will they help you hit those high and low notes, but being thoroughly warmed up gives you the feeling of being prepared for those complicated words that have to be sung in triplets and rapid eighth and sixteenth notes that can make or break your overall performance.

I have said many times already that voiceover is analogous to music. I confidently state without a doubt that most speaking, breathing, and interpretation skills work and apply to both the speaking and singing genres equally. They are one and the same. Below is a great tongue twister for singers.

Speak with pace—the faster the better but please be clear.

The Singer

Singer singer pleasure bringer sing and speak a real humdinger

Sing the words and split the verbs flip your tongue and be superb

Singer singer pleasure bringer sing and speak a real humdinger!

EXERCISES

Singers (and voiceover actors) can warm up by doing the following exercises. Repeat them until you feel warmed up enough to start singing or speaking.

- ❏ Start by rubbing the tension out of your face.
- ❏ Take your hands and massage your jaws.
- ❏ Go up to just under your ears and rub briskly.
- ❏ Take your thumb and massage the muscle under your chin.
- ❏ Yawn a couple of times.

LIP TRILLS

My vocal teacher use to call this the "bubble." It's a great warm-up exercise for singers and anyone using their voice for public speaking. To make this exercise work, you need to imagine that you are underwater and you are blowing bubbles. When you blow the air out from your lips, add voice to this process so you get a *brbrbrbr* sound as your lips vibrate. Make sure that you are breathing properly and using your diaphragm correctly.

THE SIREN

With this exercise, I want you to concentrate on actually emulating the sound of a siren. Start with the lowest note in your vocal range and sing up to the highest note like a siren. Your mouth should be open. Your tongue should be totally relaxed. Go up and go back down very gently, do not shout. Now, do the same thing with your mouth closed and humming.

CHAPTER **23**

Prepare for Your Next Speech

DO YOU HAVE A SPEAKING ENGAGEMENT? GET PREPARED with a tongue twister that will help you enunciate and communicate your content with a flare that can only be achieved with a proper warm-up. Whether your speech is long or short, energetic or laidback, you will need to warm-up properly.

"Speech is the voice of the heart."
—Anna Quindlen

Read the following tongue twister that not only gets your mouth muscles loose, but also speaks to what you want to accomplish with your speech. Read at the same pace that you plan to read your speech. Also, remember that we speak approximately 150 words per minute, so three doubled-spaced, typewritten pages will take about five minutes to deliver. Of course, that is all based on how quickly you speak.

The tongue twisters in this book will help you develop the skills to meet any time restraints or extensions.

Stand

As I stand splendidly and strongly before the crowd
I speak with sincere simplicity soft and loud
Luminous lively long and short
Positive passionate punctuation to retort
And respectively respond to the superlative sound
Of the timely transparent thunderous applause
They like me they love me
They react to my call
Preparation dedication
Did well stand tall

Did you notice the positive lines throughout the preceding poem/tongue twister? Be sure to include this type of positive rhetoric whenever you prepare for a speech. From now on, your process should be:

- Come up with your speech topic
- Speech outline
- Write your speech
- Read the Stand poem/tongue twister

- ❏ Edit your speech
- ❏ Practice your speech
- ❏ Read the Stand poem/tongue twister
- ❏ Practice your speech
- ❏ Critique your read
- ❏ Read the Stand poem/tongue twister
- ❏ Practice your speech until you are completely confident

Now, go out there and give a dynamic award-winning speech!

"Proper Planning and Preparation
Prevents Poor Performance."
—Stephen Keague

Section 6

Enhance Your Voiceover Career

"Progress lies not in enhancing what is,
but in advancing toward what will be."
—KHALIL GIBRAN

"I have never ever met a hard worker who wasn't successful. There simply is no other possible outcome."
—Rodney Saulsberry

CHAPTER **24**

Building a Successful Career

I SINCERELY HOPE YOU HAVE NOT ONLY LEARNED A LOT throughout the first five sections of this book, but that you also had fun reading the tongue twisters and doing the warm-ups. Now, it's time to transform what you've learned into income.

We've talked a lot about the "show" part; now it's time to talk about the business part. But first things first: the secret to success in voiceover, as in any endeavor, is to believe in yourself. If you can dream it you can do it.

Look in the mirror and **smile** while vocalizing and doing tongue twisters. Studies surrounding what's called the "facial feedback theory" suggest that the expressions on your face can actually encourage your brain to register certain emotions. By looking in the mirror and smiling every day, you might feel happier with yourself and more self-confident.

AVOID BEING A PERFECTIONIST

Perfectionism can paralyze you and keep you from accomplishing your goals. It's okay to strive for perfection but don't beat yourself up for not achieving it. Trust me, in the process of trying to achieve perfection, you are better off and will get closer to reaching your goals.

Let me share some of the reasons why the top moneymakers in the voiceover industry are the top money makers in the voiceover industry. They control their voiceover destinies and they will be successful for many years to come because:

- *They think they're supposed to be successful.* What you think about, you bring about.
- *They have focus.* Wear blinders as you race to the target that is success.
- *They take care of their instrument.* Take good care of your voice and health.
- *They have a plan.* Define your goals and then decide on a course of action.
- *They have no fear of failure.* You might not make it, but do dare to try.
- *They have extreme confidence.* Believe that no matter what, you will prevail.
- *They practice.* Your habitual practicing makes being excellent a habit.
- *They are punctual.* On time beats being late every time, but too early is annoying.
- *They are professional.* Conduct yourself in a business-like manner in the studio.
- *They have direction.* Your positive direction gets you where you want to be.

- *They know who they are.* You have to find your "money voice."
- *They have omnipotence.* Achieve unlimited "power" in your attitude.
- *They hunger for knowledge.* You're always a student. Take more VO classes.
- *They adjust to change.* Be aware of changes in the voiceover industry.

If you strive to possess all of the attributes above, you too will be in control of *your voiceover destiny* and successful for many years to come.

BUILDING A BLUEPRINT FOR SUCCESS

Instead of thinking about what you *don't* want, focus on what you do want. If you were playing darts, you'd focus on the bull's eye—not on all of the places you *don't* want to hit. Likewise, you need to focus on the jobs you want to get—genres that you are right for and not jobs that you can't possibly do. If the audition calls for a basso bass voice, don't audition for it if you have a high tenor voice.

Consider:
- How you will appear to others you meet.
- What kinds of equipment you will buy for your home studio.
- What kinds of jobs you want

And then focus on these.

> "A goal without a plan is just a wish."
> —Herm Edwards

Before building a new home from the ground up, you need a plan that is also known as a blueprint. You need the same thing when you are building a new or improved voiceover career.

Here are a few things that must be included in your blueprint:

RESEARCH

- The Internet is your friend
- Read voiceover books

TRAINING

- Attend voiceover workshops
- Take acting classes
- Take singing classes
- Take improvisation classes
- Join The Consultant's Club (my subscription consulting services, see page 187)

PRACTICE

- Constantly read copy
- Practice tongue twisters
- Do daily vocal warm-ups

DEMO
- Create a vocal business card
- A commercial demo should always be your first demo
- Let A1Voice Demo Productions produce your next demo

AGENT
You must have representation. There are several agencies that represent talent all over the country and on the Internet.

WEBSITE
Establish your own website to promote your talents and brand (which is you).

GET THE RIGHT NUTRIENTS
Just like you need to ingest proper nutrients to stay physically healthy, you also need positive nutrients to develop, nourish, stimulate, and maintain a healthy mind. Positive nutrients will sustain you in good and bad times during your career.

"In voiceover, you are what you learn. What do YOU want to be?"
—Rodney Saulsberry

Here are some ways to add nutrients to your voiceover career:

Put together a strong team. 1. Find an agent you believe in, and who believes in you. 2) Find a financial adviser you trust for advice and to take good care of your money. 3) Interact with friends who stimulate you in a positive way. 4) Get rid of people in your life who bring you down. 5) Find your signature voice and stop trying to excel in areas that don't suit your talent.

Elevate your game. Once you have purged the negativity that stops you from being successful, and added positive nutrients, you can set higher goals, face new challenges, work harder than ever before, and really build your self-confidence.

Give praise to those around you. A great way to boost your self-confidence is to boost the confidence of the people around you.

Your sessions can be a haven of joy if you use positive reinforcement when interacting with the people. This applies to workshops too. When you are in a class, it helps to encourage and praise the other participants. This behavior will more often than not bring about positive consequences, i.e., the more sweetness you give out, the more sweetness you will receive. Be sincere in your praise, not forced. If you deliver praise when it is warranted, it will not come off as overt.

Take the time to praise the engineer and the director. You can even compliment the other talent in the session when it's appropriate to do so. Some people call this bribery or flattery. Maybe it is, but the purpose of this behavior is to make the workplace a happy and joyous environment for everyone.

I'm not asking you to be a kiss-ass—just suggesting that if

you're nice to others, they will be nice to you and everyone's self-confidence will be improved in the process.

Know your subject. If you are well-versed in your field, you will be more confident. In other words, if you have knowledge you have power, which in turn gives you self-confidence. Therefore you must always: Practice, practice, practice; learn, learn, learn; study, study, study; create, create, create; and grow, grow, grow.

The Five W's. This is an exercise you should do every day to get into a positive frame of mind. Go through these questions and answers each morning before you start your day, filling in your own specific information if you want to.

WHO are you? (State your name.)

WHAT are you? (A working voiceover artist.)

WHEN are you a voiceover artist? (Right now.)

WHERE are you a voiceover artist? (In studios throughout the country.)

WHY are you a voiceover artist? (Because I love it!)

When you put it all together, it will sound like this:

"Who am I? I am Rodney. What am I? I am a working voiceover artist. When? Right now. Where? In studios all over the country. Why? Because I love it!"

Go over this list until you are ready to start your day.

CHAPTER **25**

Setting Career Goals

WHERE WOULD YOU LIKE TO BE IN YOUR VOICEOVER career in three years? Perhaps your goals are similar to these.

Year One: Set up a complete, functional home studio.

Year Two: Get agent representation.

Year Three: Become a working voiceover artist.

"A good teacher can inspire hope, ignite the imagination, and instill a love of learning."
—Brad Henry

TEN TIPS TO IGNITE YOUR CAREER

If you want to ignite your voiceover career and boost your self-confidence:

1. Be creative.
2. Think about the big picture.
3. Keep an open mind.
4. Take time to make time.
5. Give yourself the opportunity to be yourself.
6. Be true to yourself and others.
7. Define your intentions.
8. Stay positive.
9. Keep it simple.
10. Never underestimate your power.

"Networking is an essential part of building wealth."
—Armstrong Williams

NETWORKING

Don't be a loner. Keep your ear to the ground so that you can hear about potential work through your friends and colleagues in the business. Attend industry parties and pass out your business card or demo when appropriate.

But that's just the start of networking! In order to get work, you must also do the following:

1. **Establish an online presence.** You need your own website, and you should consider joining pay-to-play websites such as Voices.com and Voice123.com. Utilizing Facebook and YouTube is always a plus.

2. **Obtain an industry contact list.** You can compile one by gathering information from the following websites:

    Voice Over Resource Guide (www.voiceoverresourceguide.com)

    LA 411 (www.la411.com)

    NY 411.com (www.newyork411.com)

3. **Have a plan.** A goal without a plan is just a dream. If you fail to plan, you plan to fail. Focus your energy and actions. Make a list of five contacts to pursue each week.

4. **Have the desire to be successful.** When there is a will, there is a way. If you really want it, you will get work. Don't just say it—do it!

5. **Never give up.** A quitter will never win and a winner will never quit. Remember, it takes time to achieve goals. Hard work will always open the door to success.

6. **Stick to what works.** If something that you are doing is bringing you positive results, don't change. Remember, if it isn't broke, don't break it.

You can't do any better than well done."
—Oprah Winfrey

PLANTING THE SEEDS

Every day you must do things that lead to work; I call this the "planting seeds method." Do not expect to get a yes on the first, second, or even third attempt to hire an agent or manager. You should be willing to plant a lot of seeds before you land one—if that is what it takes to reach your goal.

So you didn't get the job you auditioned for ... how long does it take to audition for something else? If you keep auditioning and auditioning, eventually you will get a job.

Be willing to plant many seeds—and audition over and over and over again.

The fact is: your probability of success goes up when you plant more seeds, not just because you are planting more seeds, but because every new seed you plant is likely a better seed than the last one. You are likely to learn more from your last seed and become better at networking, writing emails, cold-calling, interpreting copy, or whatever it is you are planting.

So please, as you pursue your voiceover career, don't give up. Don't get discouraged, just plant more seeds!

START AN EMAIL CAMPAIGN

Create a marketing plan that focuses on your strengths. If you are good at reading narration, emphasize that fact in your emails. Create a plan specifically around what you are good at and what you enjoy doing.

GET YOUR MESSAGE RIGHT

Ask yourself the following questions: What is my brand? Do I have a hook? Do I have any slogans? What is my unique selling point? What is different about my voice and sound?

IDENTIFY YOUR TARGET AUDIENCE

Make a list of the best people to send your emails to. Do your research and compile a comprehensive list. If you contact the wrong people you are only wasting your time.

As a voiceover artist your audience consists of casting directors, producers, and anyone who has the potential to hire you for voiceover work.

You don't need to spend a lot of money to put together a successful marketing campaign. As a matter of fact, you don't have to spend much money at all. All you need to do is combine proper research with a strong desire to win and you will succeed.

CHAPTER **26**

Be a Winner

ALL OF US HAVE HAD VICTORIES IN OUR LIVES. EVEN THE smallest victory counts as a positive moment. Think about what that positive moment felt like, and rekindle the feeling.

When you are faced with disappointment or feel defeated, recall that victory feeling. If you can do this, you can force yourself to eliminate negative energy. The ability to get in touch with the winner in you is necessary for dealing with the constant rejection you will face in the voiceover industry. It's comforting to know that if you can think about the good times in your past, you can ease your present pain more quickly.

SET A PERSONAL BAR

Your competition is you. The quicker you grasp this concept, the quicker you will start winning. It's okay to admire others. But it is not okay to let them set your standards of achievement.

Everyone is different and marches to his or her own drum. No one can be you better than you. Cultivate your own style. Find your signature voice. Set your own bar and rise to it.

Be the best that you can be. That's good enough.

TO BE A WINNER …

You have to be able to withstand failure. You must have courage and tenacity. You must be able to withstand humiliation. You must know how to get back up, again and again and again. You need to break free of limitations

WINNERS ARE …

Self-confident, optimistic, healthy, and hard working.

THE SCIENCE OF SMALL WINS

When you set goals for yourself, start out with ones you know are possible. When you accomplish these goals it will give you a sense of satisfaction. Now, because of this win, you feel more ready and prepared to accomplish a bigger and more challenging goal. When you succeed at that one, you will be ready for the next …

TAKE CARE OF YOUR HEALTH

Take care of your vocal health and properly warm up

before reading copy. Treat your body with the proper care that it truly deserves.

Remember to always work harder on yourself than on anything else in your life. Promise yourself to always maintain a fit body and treat it better than you do anything else. Once you do this, you will be on track to develop the mindset of a **real winner**!

IT TAKES TIME

Have you ever heard the phrase "Rome wasn't built in a day"? This is so true when it comes to your career. The process of reaching your goals takes hard work and time. It's a fact that a successful professional voiceover artist earns more than the average employee who works a nine-to-five job. There are many lucrative opportunities available—be patient and work for it.

FIND YOUR VOICE AND WHAT YOU DO BEST

Who are you vocally? Have you ever thought about that? You need to find your own voice. Learn what your sound is, your vocal quality and range. When you define the aspects of your voice that are unique to you, you can develop your own style.

Experienced voiceover performers probably already know this. Newcomers need to read a lot of copy from every genre to determine which ones they do best. Once you establish what you do best, then you know what kind of work to go after. If it's commercials, then go after commercials. If it's promos and audiobooks, go after promos and audiobooks. Make sure that you are realistic. If you are not good at medical narration, don't waste your time going after medical narration.

Find the desire of your heart, something you are truly passionate about, as well as good at, and then figure out how to make money doing it.

BUILD YOUR BRAND AND STAND OUT IN THE VOICEOVER CROWD

The importance of *branding* has exploded in recent years—both on the Internet and in the workplace.

Websites are the new business cards. Not only do they (your personal website as well as the industry-sponsored sites) house your demos, they also have your bio, resume, and other vital information that a potential client will need when they are considering your services.

Your website among other things should include: a list of high-profile clients that you have worked for in the past; positive testimonials from those clients and other customers; prestigious awards that you've won; and interviews that you've done on radio, television, or print.

"It's so easy to be average. To hell with that, you want to be great!"

–Urban Meyer

THE POWER OF POSITIVE THINKING

The job market can be highly competitive. With so many other people possessing the same level of talent and experience, you need to have a mental edge. You can have that edge with the power of positive thinking.

Voiceover performers who are negative and depressive don't work as much as performers with a positive attitude. Positive voiceover actors also seem to have positive energy and endless enthusiasm to achieve their goals.

Having a positive attitude will increase your ability to find other positive people who will encourage you, hire you, and generally want to be your friend.

A positive mind anticipates happiness and a favorable outcome.

I know it's not easy, but try to always visualize only favorable and beneficial situations. Use positive words in your thoughts and when talking with others. Disregard any feelings of laziness or a desire to quit. If you persevere in the present, you will transform the way your mind thinks in the future.

ANTS—AUTOMATIC NEGATIVE THOUGHTS

Negative thoughts, words, and attitudes bring up negative and unhappy moods and actions. When your mind is negative, it generates more unhappiness and negativity. This is surely the way to failure, frustration, and disappointment.

It is hard to avoid ants, but if you do avoid them, it will change your life. The sooner you start to see the sunny side as opposed to the dark side you will experience the ultimate feeling of content.

Then you can get on with the business of flourishing in your career. Why not approach everything from a positive point of view? Try to find the positive in every situation.

IMPROVE YOUR ENVIRONMENT

Do you have an office? Is it comfortable? Does it inspire you to work? Do you have a home studio? Does it bring out the best of you when you read copy? Your environment is very important. Make sure it is conducive to helping you produce the best performance every time.

WATCH YOUR LABELS

What do you call yourself? An actor, a voiceover actor, or an entrepreneur? Or maybe you are all of the above? The bottom line is, whichever title you choose, the one that makes you feel good and be more productive is the one that you should use. How you label yourself is important to your overall positive attitude about yourself.

DON'T COMPARE YOURSELF TO OTHERS

It is human nature to compare ourselves to other voiceover talent in sound, style, and general attitude. The key is to try not to compare and instead accept and embrace who you are.

Accept your own voice, style, and personality, and accept your career. This will give you the power to be more unique and create your own persona—your own brand.

You're only human! Remember, life is for living not worrying. Be positive about you!

LAUGH MORE

Laughter is great therapy. If you can find an activity that keeps a smile on your face you will definitely increase your chances of having a positive attitude.

PRACTICE YOUR CRAFT

When it comes to having a flourishing career, nothing is more important than the seed of "practice." Aristotle once said, "We are what we repeatedly do. Excellence, therefore, is not an act but a habit."

In other words, if we practice long and hard enough, it does become a habit. The excellence we arrive at in interpreting copy, reading fast tags, and other genres is a reflection of the many hours of practice that we put in.

Make excellence a habit!

Glossary

Ad lib: A line that comes from the actor that is an addition or alteration to the written script.

Alkalol: Provides natural relief from nasal congestion caused by sinusitis and allergies. Helps clean and moisturize nasal passages.

Analogous: When something is similar or comparable. Voiceover is analogous to music.

Announcer: The name applied to the voice actor who is reading the non-character copy. Some abbreviations used include ANN or ANNC on scripts.

Announcery: A slang term referring to a voiceover artist not sounding like a typical announcer but a more conversational read.

Availability: The time an actor is available for a session. Advertising employers or producers will call an agent to find out about an actor's availability.

Booking: The advertiser has hired you for a session. The client calls the actor or actor's agent to book an actor for a job.

Cadence: The rhythm of the words and phrasing when you read a piece of copy.

Call-back: A second shot at an audition. The competition is less every time you get a call-back. You are getting closer to actually getting the job.

Cold read: Seeing copy and reading it for the first without opportunity for a rehearsal.

Conjunction: The action of two things occurring at the same time.

Copy: Also known as the script. It is the text for a spot.

De-esser: A piece of recording/sound equipment used to remove excess sibilance.

Dialogue: Copy within a script written for two or more actors.

Dry mouth: A situation or condition where you have very little saliva.

Ellipsis: Three periods in a row that usually signify a pause …

Engineer: Person who operates the audio equipment during the voiceover session.

Fluctuation: How often a voice goes up or down, also known as inflection.

Groove: Establishing an interpretation tempo while reading written text.

ISDN: Integrated Services Digital Network. Special high-quality lines that allow voice recording to be digitally transmitted from one recording facility to another throughout the world.

Lip trills: Vocal exercises that combine the lips, breathing, and singing making a bubbling sound and movement.

Lisp: A speech defect or mannerism characterized by mispronunciation of the sounds *s* and *z* as *th*.

Mic: Microphone.

Mouth noise: The mouth clicks, lip smacks, and pops a microphone picks up from a dry mouth.

MP3: The compression of audio signals in a file extension that can be sent through an email while maintaining a quality that is ready for broadcast in the minds of many.

Non-announcerish: Another slang term referring to a voiceover artist not sounding like a typical announcer but a more conversational read.

Off axis: Speaking off mic to the right or the left of the microphone.

Over-the-top: Direction that makes the copy sound larger than life, requiring the actor to overact.

Pace: The speed in which an actor reads and phrases copy.

Personalization: Memorizing your own personal favorite tongue twisters.

Phonation: to produce vocal sounds and especially speech.

Pick-ups: Re-do some lines or add new lines in a voiceover session.

Plosives: Words that begin with P, T, or B or ny consonant or combination of consonants that cause popping.

Pop: When the voice hits the mic too hard. This happens most often with plosive words.

Pop filter: A foam cover enveloping the mic or a nylon windscreen in front of the mic. Lessens popping. Also known as a popper stopper.

Post-production: Also known as post. The work done after the voice talent has finished recording the session. You can take out breaths or mouth clicks in post-production.

Processor: An apparatus or software that treats or converts the sound of the voice in post-audio production.

Ramp-Up: Improvisational Ad-libbing at the beginning before you read the written dialog.

Read Through Rehearsal: The animation or video-game cast does a full reading of the script before it is recorded.

Roller coaster: Going up and down with your phrasing while reading copy.

Sibilance: A drawn out or excessive "S" sound during speech. The state or quality of a hissing sound. A sibilant speech sound, such as English *s*, *sh*, or *zh*.

Signature: An actor's most employable voice. The sound you can always refer to. The specific quality of your voice that makes it unique.

Spot: A commercial.

Tag: Information placed at the end of a commercial containing a date, time, phone number, website address, legal disclaimer, etc. A different announcer sometimes reads the tag.

Tempo: The speed at which you read the copy. The pace.

Trailer: A commercial that promotes a film or video release.

Vignettes: A brief, evocative description, account, or episode.

Vocal folds: The vocal folds, also known commonly as vocal cords or voice reeds, are composed of twin in-foldings of mucous membrane stretched horizontally, from back to front, across the larynx. They vibrate modulating the flow of air being expelled from the lungs during phonation.

Windscreen: A pop filter or pop stopper.

Bibliography and References

Aaron Matthew. Your Personal Singing Guide; http://your-personal-singing-guide.com/lip-trill.html

Alburger, James. *The Art of Voice Acting: The Craft and Business of Performing Voiceover*. Focal Press, 2010.

Ciccarelli, David and Ciccarelli, Stephanie. *Voice Acting For Dummies*. For Dummies. 2013.

I Know That Voice (DVD). Dundee Entertainment and Cinovative. Executive producer John Di Maggio, Video Services Corp., 2014.

Peak Fitness (www.mercola.com)

Saulsberry, Rodney. *Step Up to the Mic: A Positive Approach to Succeeding in Voice Overs*. Tomdor Publishing, 2007.

Saulsberry, Rodney. *You Can Bank on Your Voice: Your Guide to a Successful Career in Voice Overs*. Tomdor Publishing, 2004.

The Singers Resource (www.thesingersresource.com)

About the Author

RODNEY SAULSBERRY is one of the most sought after voiceover talents and voiceover coaches in the world. A two-time NAACP Image Award Nominee, Rodney has given voice to many commercial campaigns that include Zatarain's, Toyota, Alpo, Twix, Colgate; and many movie trailers such as *Red Tails, How Stella Got Her Groove Back, Dumb & Dumberer, The Best Man,* and *Friday.*

As an announcer, Rodney has worked on the NAACP Image Awards and The Essence Awards television specials. He is the author of two other books, *You Can Bank on Your Voice* and *Step Up to the Mic.*

Join the Consultant's Club

ARE YOU INTERESTED IN ONE-ON-ONE CONSULTATION and training? Since 2004, when I released my first book, *You Can Bank on Your Voice*, I have taught numerous workshops around the country, held many tele-classes, and coached hundreds of students, many who now have successful careers using their voice.

I genuinely love helping others. I love to teach. Your success after my tutelage brings me much joy. Each time you work, vicariously, I do too.

That is why I created the Consultant's Club. I want the opportunity to consult with you on a regular basis. I am here to help you with your demos, auditioning, marketing, home studio, motivation, positive mental attitude, and your career as you pursue your voiceover goals.

What is unique about joining the Consultant's Club is that everything you get is tailor fitted to you. All levels of experience are welcome. My techniques and guidance are highly functional for the newbie as well as seasoned professionals. You will be on the cutting edge of everything that is going on in the voiceover community with a Consultant's Club membership. This is your chance to be part of a group that is getting expert advice and feedback from an insider consultant who is working every day in this highly competitive industry.

When you get advice you want to know that you are getting the real scoop.

After you join, we will schedule your first consultation with me where we will address your personal needs. This will be our most important session because it will tell us exactly how we should proceed with your specific needs as we go forward.

You will have access to password protected pages on my website where you can watch educational videos along with brief text tutorials that will help you sharpen your skills. Some of my most popular YouTube videos will be there, along with text that only you can get as a member of this club.

Every month you will have access to voiceover training videos that cover subjects like narration, promotion, motivation, marketing, branding, audiobooks, Internet voice imaging, and how to get started in the business. Other Membership Highlights:

- A free copy of my book *Tongue Twisters and Vocal Warm-Ups*
- One personal 30-minute phone session per month
- One 1-hour group coaching phone session per month
- 50% off a One-on-One 1-hour Voiceover Coaching Session
- Critiques of your demos, auditions, and works in progress
- Access to my Conference Call archives
- Blog posts dedicated to members only
- Re-edit your current demo. Rearrange it to be competitive in today's market (1 demo)
- Monthly guest expert interviews
- Monthly educational video and audio training modules.
  If you have any questions, just pick up the phone and call me at (818) 207-2682.

To sign up for the low price of $69.95 per month, go directly to my website: www.rodneysaulsberry.com

As your consultant, adviser, and coach, I will provide support when you need it.

I Want to Hear from You

Do you have some challenging tongue twisters or vocal warm-ups that you want to share? Please send them to me and I will post them on my blog, in a newsletter, or my next book! If you have any unusual remedies for a sore throat or stuffy nose, email those remedies to me at rodtalks@pacbell.net. Or, you can mail them to me at:

Tomdor Publishing
P.O. Box 1735
Agoura Hills, CA 91376

ADDITIONAL CONTACT INFORMATION
www.rodneysaulsberry.com

Agency Representation:

WME (William Morris Endeavor Talent Agency)
310-859-4289
9601 Wilshire Blvd., Suite 3,
Beverly Hills, CA 90210
www.wma.com

Information Distribution

Whenever you get a hold of some really good information, the honorable thing to do is to share it with others. One of the primary functions of well-intentioned human beings is to distribute information. That is the reason I write books: I believe in information distribution.

The concept is similar to the term "pay it forward" but it's a little more detailed than that. It calls for you to not just do a kind deed for one or two people, but for many people. Not just once but forever. In other words, tell your friends about this book. And better yet, purchase it and send them a copy. Your job is to distribute this information to as many people as you can.

How can you do that? There are three methods that you can incorporate into your daily routine that will be effective:

1. Take the time to compile a list of people you think would benefit from owning this book. You will be surprised by the large amount of people that you come up with when you list your friends and acquaintances in voiceover, music, and business. All these people use their voices in some way or another to generate income.

2. Create a comprehensive list of their addresses, both email and snail mail. A list of phone numbers for those who you want to talk with about the book. This list should go far beyond your inner circle of actors and singers. Here is a list of other professions who might be interested in this book. Perhaps you know someone in one or more of these fields.

Public Relations, Receptionists, Sales Persons, Public Speakers, Speech Teachers, Acting Teachers, Singing Teachers, Radio Jocks, and Auctioneers.

Spread the word about this book in social media. If you have a website, post it there. Use Facebook, Twitter, Pinterest and LinkedIn to distribute this pertinent information.

How did you find out about this book? Use that same method to impart information distribution. Remember, when you tell somebody they tell somebody and so on and so on. And soon it becomes, as they say in the cyber world, "viral."

Thank you!

www.ingramcontent.com/pod-product-compliance
Lightning Source LLC
Chambersburg PA
CBHW020800160426
43192CB00006B/395